One Pastor
Twelve Steps

Preaching My Way Through the Valley of the Shadow of Addiction

Jim Dant

Scripture quotations are from New Revised Standard Version Bible, copyright © 1989 National Council of the Churches of Christ in the United States of America. Used by permission. All rights reserved.

Published in Macon, Georgia, by Faithlab, faithlab.com.

Library of Congress Cataloging-in-Publication Data is available.

ISBN 978-0-9839863-4-8

Printed in the United States of America

For Holly

(...and all of Bill's friends who have become my friends.)

ACKNOWLEDGMENTS

One of the first things we learn in Alanon is "the three c's"—you didn't cause it, you can't control it, and you can't cure it. The same truths we attach to addiction can be applied to the writing of this manuscript. I'm not the source of every idea in this book—I didn't cause all of these thoughts to emerge. I wasn't completely in control of the production of this manuscript—a host of wonderful people brought their insights and angles to everything from title and cover design to content and structure. And finally, I can't cure whatever ills one might find here—even with multiple sets of eyes (and some wonderfully perceptive minds) applying their talents to this document, there are sure to be some mistakes here and there. This barely concerns me. When you've traveled the road of addiction, you become quite receptive to grace, generous with grace, and keenly aware of the constant need for it.

With that said, allow me to thank a few individuals who have made the publication of this book possible.

Jim E. encouraged me to attend my first Alanon meeting. If he hadn't become "my pastor" at a critical time in my life, I'm quite certain my journey from the pit would have taken much longer...if I had found the strength to make the journey at all. Along with Jim, all other Alanon members in the Middle Georgia area deserve a word of gratitude. Their welcome and wisdom ushered me toward serenity during an insane time of life.

Terry Cantwell is my sponsor in Alanon and has served as my spiritual director for the last couple of years. His insight and patience have been invaluable...not just with regard to living amid addiction... but in all other areas of life as well.

Jean Trotter and Carol Brown lent their editorial eyes to the manuscript. Their knowledge of verbs and nouns and clauses and conjunctions helped clean up my messy mix of doodles and scribbles.

Joy Yee is a colleague beyond colleague, friend beyond friend, and sister beyond sister. During those inevitable "plateau moments" in the writing process, she became an encourager, reader and advisor...listening for my voice within each line and helping me shape the final copy.

And finally, I can never take for granted the excellent team of baristas at the Barnes and Noble Café in Macon, Georgia's Shoppes at Rivers Crossing. Katybug and the rest of the crew have kept the coffee pouring...even when the words weren't.

TABLE OF CONTENTS

INTRODUCTION

This only happens to other people. And in the role of pastor, I had seen it happen a lot. I had seen it only weeks prior to my own experience...

The voice of our church's Administrative Assistant jarred me out of a morning daydream, "Dr. Dant, Jim E. is on line 1. Do you have time to speak with him?"

She had given me his full name. (I'm leaning toward anonymity in these pages.) I recognized the name but did not know the man. He was a member of the congregation I pastored, but I could not recall ever seeing him in worship. I dreaded answering the call and taking responsibility—or making an excuse—for having never contacted him during my decade as his pastor.

"Jim Dant," I politely said as I answered the phone.

"Dr. Dant, you don't know me." he responded, "I haven't been the best member of the church, but I need to talk to you if you have some time. I'm in the middle of a situation that has caused me to ask some questions I can't answer."

I sat silent on my side of the phone. Taking a deep breath I said, "Well, I haven't been the best pastor either...since I've never called to find out why you don't attend. Let's just call it even and go get lunch."

We met at a local "catfish house" and loaded up on the healthiest fried fish, french fries, and cole slaw that our little city has to offer. After wiping our hands of the feast's residuals, Jim told me his story. In short, he had a child who had fallen prey to the disease of addiction. The people and places he had encountered while trying to save his child were quite foreign to the upper middle class context to which he was accustomed. The pain he expressed in watching his child spiral further and further into this destructive lifestyle made my chest and stomach ache. I wished I hadn't eaten anything. Remarkably, while his pain was deep and real, he seemed to be handling it extremely well. He had a sense of peace and personhood that transcended what I imagined the parent of an addict might enjoy. In fact, our discussions did not exclusively revolve around addiction. The whole experience had thrust him into thinking—thinking about God and life and free will and suffering and choices and salvation. We talked a long time. And then we both went back to work.

Driving back to the church office, I said a prayer for Jim and his family. And then, quite selfishly, voiced a prayer for myself and my family, "Dear God, I hope that never happens to me."

Six weeks later I was riding a motorcycle from central Georgia to a state park on the western edge of the state. A friend and I were determined to ride our motorcycles to every state park in the state. Stopping for a sip of water, I checked my cell phone. I had missed a call from the high school where my children attended classes. I returned the call, was promptly transferred to the principal's office and was told one of my children had confessed to being high on cocaine while at school.

It is not my business to share my child's story with you. That story is my child's to share. I do want to share my struggle with you, however. I am the "family member or friend" of an addict. There are more of us than there are addicts. There are more persons struggling with addicts than there are addicts struggling with addiction. We need help.

I should have seen it coming. In short, my child had been spotted smoking pot downtown once; I gave a lecture and wrote it off as adolescent, rebellious behavior. I saw a "pill" in her purse a few weeks later. I confronted her—she blamed it on needing relief from a headache at school. I confronted the family of the child that sold her the pill—a doctor in our community whose child had raided his cabinet. He didn't believe his child was involved. I showed him a text message from his child to mine stating "...some pinks would be available at school the next day...." He told me his child said they were talking about construction paper for a project. I told him my child said they were talking about drugs. He said my child was lying. I told him it's more likely the "construction paper" story was a lie compared to a "drug confession" story. He disagreed. I had finally found someone in deeper denial than myself.

My point? I kept seeing hints of my child's diversion from sobriety, but found it hard to believe an addiction was looming. By the time I received the call from the principal's office, my child was using to the degree that an overdose was not only possible, but probable. I became determined to control every minute of her life. I regulated her every move. I drove her to school...walked her to classes...picked her up....prayed for her...spied on her...and still...she used every day. Every day.

Giving this much attention to my child's life caused my life to crumble. Neither my mind nor my body was at work as often as it needed to be. Worry dominated my thoughts. I was surviving...but barely. Not knowing what to do, I remembered the only "sane parent of an addict" I knew, Jim E. I called Jim and asked if he was up for another catfish lunch. He was.

In the course of our conversation, Jim encouraged me to attend Alanon—the sister 12-Step program of Alcoholics Anonymous (AA). While AA focuses on helping alcoholics find sobriety, Alanon's mission is to help the family and friends of alcoholics discover and maintain serenity—whether the alcoholic is drinking or not. The next week, I sheepishly made my way to an Alanon meeting. I crept in...hoping no one would know me. Entering the room, I stared at the floor and made my way to an empty chair. Finally, I lifted my head and looked around; I knew a third of the people in the room—and they knew me. I attended meetings for almost three weeks before I said a word. Honestly, I sat in my chair...tissue box in my lap...and cried during the meetings.

As the days and weeks rolled on, however, I found hope and strength in the room. It was a hope and a strength I would need.

Weeks before my child's graduation, I received another call from the principal's office. I drove to the school, parked my car, walked into the office and saw the child I loved...handcuffed and seated in front of a standing police officer. The residue of Robitussin and cocaine were visible on the front of my child's shirt. Tears were dripping down my child's cheeks.

Looking up at me, my child fearfully yet hopefully said, "Dad, I know you can fix this."

I paused...for a long time. My child was right. A few words with the principal and a few more words with law enforcement and a "smack on the hand" probably would have been her sentence.

I finally replied, "I can...but I won't."

The police officer escorted my dreams down the hallway.

I could have never made that decision—said those words—without Alanon. I would not have known what to do had it not been for those sacred 12 Steps.

Three months later my child had completed rehab...completed her high school course work...and was completely unsure if sobriety would be the final description of life. Three years later, my child was still clean and sober. It took me that long to finally infuse my journey into the medium with which I most often communicated with my faith community—the sermon. Knowing that the 12 Steps were applicable to more than just the disease of addiction, I decided to preach on each of the steps during the twelve Sundays of the summer. It was the first summer in over two decades of pastoring that I did not take a vacation. I did not want to miss a Sunday. Many parishioners felt the same way.

This book is the gist of those Sunday morning sermons. There is no way any one of the 12 Steps can be adequately parsed in the limited parameter of a sermon. Each "word" of each step has been the fodder of hundreds of hours of meditation and conversation within the rooms of anonymous recovery groups. These sermons are not exhaustive, but they are my thoughts after an exhausting journey through the valley of the shadow of addiction. They are a portion of the experience, strength, and hope I have found in working the 12 Steps. I hope they bring some strength and hope to the difficult experiences of your life as well....

CRAWDADS ANONYMOUS

Psalm 38:1-15

STEP 1

We admitted we were powerless over alcohol and that our lives had become unmanageable.

O Lord, do not rebuke me in your anger, or discipline me in your wrath. For your arrows have sunk into me, and your hand has come down on me. There is no soundness in my flesh because of your indignation; there is no health in my bones because of my sin. For my iniquities have gone over my head; they weigh like a burden too heavy for me. My wounds grow foul and fester because of my foolishness; I am utterly bowed down and prostrate; all day long I go around mourning. For my loins are filled with burning, and there is no soundness in my flesh. I am utterly spent and crushed; I groan because of the tumult of my heart. O Lord, all my longing is known to you; my sighing is not hidden from you. My heart throbs, my strength fails me; as for the light of my eyes—it also has gone from me. My friends and companions stand aloof from my affliction, and my neighbours stand far off. Those who seek my life lay their snares; those who seek to hurt me speak of ruin, and meditate treachery all day long. But I am like the deaf, I do not hear; like the mute, who cannot speak. Truly, I am like one who does not hear, and in whose mouth is no retort. But it is for you, O Lord, that I wait; it is you, O Lord my God, who will answer.

I can tell you where David has been. Before writing this Psalm, David had spent some time on top of the world like no one else in his generation. Not bad for the runt of Jesse's litter. Small and ruddy, David had spent most of his time out in the field. Any one of his older brothers would have been a better choice by sight, but this youngest child of Jesse's ended up being anointed King of Israel. In fact, he was the most celebrated King of Israel.

It all started with a giant. David was just an errand boy delivering lunch one day to his soldier brothers who were at war. Arriving at the battlefield he heard Goliath, the Giant of the Philistines, taunting the Hebrews. David was so angered by the taunts that he got out his slingshot, reached down and picked up a few small, smooth stones, loaded one up, and let it fly. A hero was born, and David ended up on top of the world.

We've all experienced seasons of life when everything seems to go our way and nothing can go wrong. Most of us have been on top of the world at least once. This is where David was before Psalm 38. It was a great place to have been.

I can also tell you where David is now in the writing of Psalm 38. David is in the middle of a crisis. Psalm 38 is not a jubilant Psalm, nor is it one of the praise Psalms, or peaceful Psalms, or Psalms of thanksgiving. Psalm 38 is the cry of a human being in crisis.

One of my favorite writers said that if the only Psalms we ever read are the happy Psalms in the Bible, then we're leaving out two-thirds of them. I can tell you where David is right now. He is smack in the middle of a crisis. Just listen to the language: "There is no soundness in my flesh...there is no health in my bones...I am utterly bowed down...I mourn all day long...I am utterly spent...I am utterly crushed." In fact, David is not just in the middle of a crisis. It sounds like David has hit rock bottom. No soundness, no health, utterly bound, utterly crushed, and utterly spent. Rock bottom. I've tried to imagine the incidents in David's life that might have brought him to write a Psalm like this. It wasn't hard to find a few that would have pushed him to that point in life. First, there was the enormous guilt from his affair with Bathsheba. After the pain that he had caused his wife, the lies and murder that it took to cover it up, the reputation that he lost from the people, the disappointment that he had caused God, David realized that he was powerless to take all that back.

Then there was the death of the child that he conceived with Bathsheba. Is there anything that pushes parents further down than the realization that they are powerless to revive a child? Or maybe David wrote Psalm 38 after his battle against the mighty Ishbi-Benob. Toward the end of his life, David went out to fight another giant, because, after all, David is a giant killer, right? So he goes out before Ishbi-Benob and is ready to fight him. But this time, Ishbi-Benob just beats the stink out of David. David's mighty men have to come to his aid and drag him off the field of battle. Then they conquer Ishbi-Benob and come back to David and tell him, "You never get to fight again. If you go out to battle again, we are going to lose the light of Israel. You are too weak, too old, and too powerless. You don't get to go out anymore." David, the great giant killer, was now powerless against giants. In each of these incidents, David realized that he was powerless. He was powerless over things, powerless over people, and powerless over the circumstances in his life. Psalm 38 is not David's attempt to play at powerlessness make some sort of verbal surrender in the community of faith to make it look like he is humble and despondent. He is truly at a point where he knows in his very core, "I am powerless and my life has become unmanageable."

There are few things sillier or sadder than someone who has not yet realized how powerless he or she is. In the New Testament Jesus is brought before Pilate who asks him a series of questions. Jesus doesn't answer any of them and Pilate says to Jesus, "Don't you know I have power over your life—to set you free or crucify you?" Jesus knows better within his soul and says, "You don't have any power at all unless my Father gives it to you." It is so silly and so sad. Pilate is talking about what he is going to do, but by the time the chief priest and the scribes and the people get through screaming at him, he ends up doing everything he doesn't want to do. He is powerless.

There are few things sillier or sadder than someone who hasn't realized yet how powerless he or she is. We've been there, haven't we? We think, "If I just had enough will power, if I just had enough money or resources, if I could just find the right words, or the right good things to do. Maybe if I had more education, or better friends, or better parents, or if I could get that one big break, then...." You can fill in the blanks with all those things we think we need in our lives to retain and maintain and regain the power we think we have, and it is just silly and sad.

I used to walk home from elementary school with my brother and our two friends, Kenneth Baxter and Jed Cain. To get to my house from school, we had to cross a railroad track that had a drainage ditch beside it. One of the things we used to love to do in the spring was to save part of our lunches by wrapping up the meat and putting it in a napkin and keeping it in our pockets all day. Then we would go down to the drainage ditch after school. The crawdads lived there. Taking a piece of string, we would tie up a piece of bologna or beef, or whatever we had that day, and then put the string down in the drainage ditch and wait for tug. At that point, we'd pull it up and a crawdad would be pinching the meat. We would pull the crawdads up and take them off and put them in a bucket. That was really, really fun. The only thing more fun than catching crawdads in the drainage ditch by the railroad track was sitting there until the 4:30 train came down the track. Forgive me before I even disclose this.

We would take two crawdads and put them on the train track, one on each side of the rail. (Children don't try this at home, but adults feel free to try this—it is funny as the dickens.) The train would start coming, rumbling on the rail, and those crawdads wouldn't jump off!

Instead, they would rear up at the train with their pinchers pinching and looking fierce until the train ran them over. I promise that it's true. They thought they had the power to battle a train...assuming crawdads can think.

It is both silly and sad to see someone who has not yet realized how powerless he or she is. Someone who, in the middle of a crisis, is convinced that he or she can meet it and beat it head-on, all on his or her own. People like that just rear up at trains and wave their hands as hard as they can. It's what David might have done all the way down to rock bottom, in the middle of this 38th Psalm.

David has been on top of the world, but now he is in a crisis, at rock bottom. Given where he has been and where he is in Psalm 38, I know where David is going. He begins the Psalm with, "O Lord," and ends the Psalm with, "Lord be not far from me. Make haste to come to me and be my salvation." David has recognized his powerlessness and surrendered his sense of control. By looking outside of himself for strength, he is going to be saved, and he is going to find serenity. The church has always been diligent about articulating plans of salvation and most of us found our salvation through plans like the Roman Road, which begins in Romans 3:23—"For all have sinned and fall short of the glory of God." We are powerless. The four spiritual laws tell us, "God has a plan for all of our lives." That's law number one, but law two says, "We are powerless on our own to embrace that plan." Powerlessness. The ABCs of salvation say: "A—Admit you are a sinner, B—believe, and C—confess." In other words, admit you are powerless on your own. Salvation, sobriety, and serenity all begin with a sense of powerlessness. This really need not have anything to do with the guilt and manipulation that the church has often imposed. Powerlessness is simple, honest surrender to the fact that we are human, and that we are not God. It was Andrew Murray who wrote, "God is ready to assume full responsibility for any life that is wholly surrendered to Him." I will say that again. "God is ready to assume full responsibility for any life that is wholly surrendered to Him."

I don't know if you have ever been to the RCA building in New York City on Fifth Avenue. When you enter that building, there is a large statue of the perfectly muscular, well-proportioned, powerful man, Atlas. However, his legs are bent and he is struggling to stand with the world on his shoulders, straining under the huge weight. That is one way to live. In New York, you can also walk to the other side of Fifth Avenue to St. Patrick's Cathedral. Inside the cathedral, just behind the altar at the front of the sanctuary, there is a statue of Jesus at eight or nine years old. With no effort at all, he is holding the whole world in his right hand. That is another way to live. The question is, which way do we want to live? Straining under the weight of the world that we are powerless to control, or admitting that we are powerless and letting God hold it?

Step 1: We admitted we were powerless and that our lives had become unmanageable. I like the way Step 1 begins with "we." It is a decision and it is a surrender that each one of us has to make. And then we walk it together with God.

WHAT DO I BELIEVE?

2 Samuel 11:26—12:15

STEP 2

Came to believe that a Power greater than ourselves could restore us to sanity.

When the wife of Uriah heard that her husband was dead, she made lamentation for him. When the mourning was over, David sent and brought her to his house, and she became his wife, and bore him a son. But the thing that David had done displeased the Lord, and the Lord sent Nathan to David. He came to him, and said to him, "There were two men in a certain city, one rich and the other poor. The rich man had very many flocks and herds; but the poor man had nothing but one little ewe lamb, which he had bought. He brought it up, and it grew up with him and with his children; it used to eat of his meagre fare, and drink from his cup, and lie in his bosom, and it was like a daughter to him. Now there came a traveller to the rich man, and he was loath to take one of his own flock or herd to prepare for the wayfarer who had come to him, but he took the poor man's lamb, and prepared that for the guest who had come to him." Then David's anger was greatly kindled against the man. He said to Nathan, "As the Lord lives, the man who has done this deserves to die; he shall restore the lamb fourfold, because he did this thing, and because he had no pity.

Nathan said to David, "You are the man! Thus says the Lord, the God of Israel: I anointed you king over Israel, and I rescued you from the hand of Saul; I gave you your master's house, and your master's wives into your bosom, and gave you the house of Israel and of Judah; and if that had been too little, I would have added as much more. Why have you despised the word of the Lord, to do what is evil in his sight? You have struck down Uriah the Hittite with the sword, and have taken his wife to be your wife, and have killed him with the sword of the Ammonites. Now therefore the sword shall never depart from your house, for you have despised me, and have taken the wife of Uriah the Hittite to be your wife. Thus says the Lord: 'I will raise up trouble against you from within your own house; and I will take your wives before your eyes, and give them to your neighbour, and he shall lie with your wives in the sight of this very sun. For you did it secretly; but I will do this thing before all Israel, and before the sun.'" David said to Nathan, "I have sinned against the Lord." Nathan said to David, "Now the Lord has put away your sin; you shall not die. Nevertheless, because by this deed you have utterly scorned the Lord, the child that is born to you shall die." Then Nathan went to his house. The Lord struck the child that Uriah's wife bore to David, and it became very ill.

Came to believe that a Power greater than ourselves could restore us to sanity. "Okay, I can just skip this one." That's what I told my spiritual director when he invited me to begin working and meditating on the words in Step 2.

I started working the Twelve Steps about three years ago. Step 2 seemed unnecessary because I already believed in God. A lot. I have been baptized three times. I was baptized in a Roman Catholic Church when I was four years old. Then was baptized again as a junior high schooler at summer camp where they scare Jesus into you, because that is what they do at youth summer camp. I was baptized a third time as a senior on high school. I decided I didn't know what I was doing at four years old or fourteen years old. Of course by that criteria, I would have had to be baptized every year because I was never quite sure what I was doing the year before anyway. Faith is so dang progressive.

Came to believe that a Power greater than ourselves could re-store us to sanity? Are you kidding? I've already believed in God my whole life. I've been enamored with God since my childhood.

While most kids were collecting baseball cards, I was memo-rizing Bible verses, and wanting to be the chaplain of all the clubs in high school. I'm a preacher, for goodness' sake. I started preaching when I was in the seventh grade. I was the Youth Sunday preacher in high school, a pastor while I was still in college, a seminary student in several seminaries, and a speaker at retreats and revivals from the east coast to the west coast. Came to believe that a Power greater than ourselves could restore us to sanity. Are you kidding? I already be-lieve in God. And I have spent the greater part of my life helping other people and encouraging other people to believe in God.

One Wednesday, I was sitting in my office with a young man who claimed that he didn't believe in God anymore. So I engaged his thought the same way I had engaged a lot of other people's thoughts before him. I said, "Tell me about the God that you don't believe in." He started clipping through all of the attributes of God that people had conveyed to him over the years; the things that he thought were odd or quirky or unfair. He went on and on and on and finally he stopped and said, "That is the God I'm talking about." I smiled and responded, "I don't believe in that God either." Then I went on to tell him about a personal God who looked nothing like the God he had imagined.

Years ago, I sat across from another friend. He was a little dif-ferent. Henry was an avowed atheist. He ran the store across the river from the little church where I pastored. Henry loved telling people he didn't believe in God. He also made great liverwurst sandwiches.

One Saturday while I was there eating lunch, he was telling me, the Baptist preacher from across the river, about his wonderfully committed atheism. On the counter was a picture of a boy I recog-nized as his grandson, who happened to attend our church. "Henry, is that Ashley?" I asked. Henry said, "Yes, he is a fine boy," and I said, "Yes, he is a fine boy. Do you mind if I keep him in my prayers?" He said, "It wouldn't do you any good because there is no God." Atheist to the core...or was he? Because then I said, "No, I want to pray for God to take his life." Yep. I wish you could have seen how mad Henry got. I didn't think he was ever going to talk with me again or make me another liverwurst sandwich. He was angry. When he finally finished cursing, I said, "Henry, if there is no God than it wouldn't matter, would it? Would it really matter if I prayed that prayer every day? Or is there a possibility you believe there might just be a God?"

Came to believe that a Power greater than ourselves could restore us to sanity. I can skip that step because I've believed in God my whole life. I have spent the greater part of my life trying to help other people to believe in God. If anyone ever asked David, "Do you believe in God?" David would have screamed, "Are you kidding? Do I believe in God? I was anointed king by the great prophet Samuel! I killed a giant with just a rock and a prayer! The music of the psalms just flow out of the air and into my mind and into my hand so that I can write them down! I have gained victories and battles that didn't seem humanly possible! I have a vision for Israel to expand its borders and to build its palaces! I've even had a vision for a temple to the almighty God of Abraham, Isaac, and Jacob! Do I believe in God? I have believed in God, loved God, and served God my whole life!!!"

So when my spiritual director invited me to begin working and meditating on the words in Step 2, I quickly responded, "I can skip this one. I'm good. I already believe in God." There was a long moment of silence and then he said, "This step doesn't say you simply came to believe in a Power greater than yourself. It says you came to believe that a Power greater than yourself could restore you to sanity. If you want to work Step 2, you can't just believe in God, you have to believe that God can and will be present and powerful in your life." Oh.

You can't just believe in God. You have to believe that God can and will be present and powerful in your life.

According to one of our popular pollsters, more than 85% of Americans claim to believe in a higher power. However, our lives indicate that we are not certain that this power—this God—is really present or powerful in our lives. There is a disconnect between our belief in God's existence and our belief in God's presence. We really don't have a problem saying that we believe God exists. We're just not sure that God exists in our lives in any practical, meaningful way.

David is so far removed from this reality that he pursues an affair with Bathsheba as if there are no consequences. He pursues it as if there is no God to hold him accountable or to help him to avoid the offense. He just lives this particular moment of life without a sense of the presence of God. When Nathan the prophet confronts him with a story that is so obvious to us that it is about David, David himself doesn't get it. There is a complete disconnect between his actions and the words of God's prophet.

Step 2 is not just believing in God. Step 2 is about coming to believe that God can and will be present and powerful in our lives. David needed to know God was present enough to know exactly what was going on in his life and powerful enough to forgive everything David had done. Everything. After those harsh, truthful words from Nathan: "This is going to happen to your family, and that is going to happen in your life, and the sword is going to follow you and on and on and on," finally David said, "I have sinned against God," and immediately Nathan said, "Your sins are forgiven." God is present and powerful in David's life.

Darlene was in the tenth grade when I was her youth minister. Darlene had grown up in the church. She believed in God, was baptized, and she embraced God's presence and power in her life. One Friday afternoon, the phone rang in my home. It was Darlene and she was frantic. "I have lost those braided bands that go on the shoulder of my band uniform and I've got to be at the game in an hour." I thought to myself, "You want me to come look for them? I know I'm your youth minister, but surely it's outside of my job description to come to your house to find braided bands that go on the shoulder of your band uniform." But Darlene didn't want me to do that. She said, "No Brother Jim, I want you to pray and ask God to help me find them." I said, "Okay, I'll say a prayer after we hang up." She said, "No, I want you to pray right now, out loud, on the phone with me." Okay. This request felt like praying for a parking space, but what harm could it do? So I prayed, "God, help her find her braided bands that go on the shoulder of her band uniform, so that she won't get in trouble at the game tonight." I hung up and ten minutes later she called and said, "Thanks, I've found them. Isn't God great?" Yes, Darlene, God is great. I'm still not praying for parking places, but when I remember Darlene, I do pray that I never completely lose the child-like trust and faith that tells me God doesn't just exist, God can and will be present and powerful in my life.

I've been a bit immersed in the music of Nicole Nordeman this last year. She's a Texas-born artist who wrote a song several years ago titled, "Help Me Believe." The first verse says, " Take me back to the time when I was maybe eight or nine and I believed. When Jesus walked on waters blue and if He helped me, I could too." She longs for the time before rationale and analytical thinking when she could simply believe.

Came to believe that a power greater than ourselves could restore us to sanity. I believe that the farther we walk in faith, the fewer simple miracles we see. That's probably all about learning to trust that even when God is not seen or felt, God is there, being present and powerful. When I hear Step 2—"came to believe that a power greater than ourselves could restore us to sanity"—I know within my own heart that it's not just about affirming that God exists. It's about affirming that God wants to be present and powerful in our lives. Amen

GOD 101

Luke 8:26-39

STEP 3

Made a decision to turn our will and our lives over to the care of God as we understood Him.

Then they arrived at the country of the Gerasenes, which is opposite Galilee. As he stepped out on land, a man of the city who had demons met him. For a long time he had worn no clothes, and he did not live in a house but in the tombs. When he saw Jesus, he fell down before him and shouted at the top of his voice, 'What have you to do with me, Jesus, Son of the Most High God? I beg you, do not torment me'— for Jesus had commanded the unclean spirit to come out of the man. (For many times it had seized him; he was kept under guard and bound with chains and shackles, but he would break the bonds and be driven by the demon into the wilds.) Jesus then asked him, 'What is your name?' He said, 'Legion'; for many demons had entered him. They begged him not to order them to go back into the abyss.

Now there on the hillside a large herd of swine was feeding; and the demons begged Jesus to let them enter these. So he gave them permission. Then the demons came out of the man and entered the swine, and the herd rushed down the steep bank into the lake and was drowned.

When the swineherds saw what had happened, they ran off and told it in the city and in the country. Then people came out to see what had happened, and when they came to Jesus, they found the man from whom the demons had gone sitting at the feet of Jesus, clothed and in his right mind. And they were afraid. Those who had seen it told them how the one who had been possessed by demons had been healed. Then all the people of the surrounding country of the Gerasenes asked Jesus to leave them; for they were seized with great fear. So he got into the boat and returned. The man from whom the demons had gone begged that he might be with him; but Jesus sent him away, saying, 'Return to your home, and declare how much God has done for you.' So he went away, proclaiming throughout the city how much Jesus had done for him.

As a pastor I know that there are times when people's confidence in me far exceeds my abilities. Parishioners come to church, follow my leadership, listen to my words, digest my thoughts and prayers, and allow me to walk with them through various crises. I'm thankful for the affirmation and trust. But I know that at times their confidence far exceeds my abilities. A few months ago, a mom came into my office and said, "Do you mind if I bring my young boy to talk with you?" I said, "Not at all. What is the problem?" She said, "He has some questions about God—where God came from, what God looks like, how God can be everywhere at the same time." I said, "What have you told him so far?" She said, "I told him to ask you because Mr. Jim knows *everything* about God." See what I mean?

I do not know everything about God. In fact, the older I get, the further along the journey of faith I move, the more time I spend in prayer with God, and the more time I spend in scripture reading about God, the less I feel I know about God. And, what I do know sounds pretty simple. Things like: **I know I'm not God.** That might sound really obvious to you, but since the days of Adam and Eve, most of us have attempted to be the God of our own lives. If we didn't think we were God, then Step 3 wouldn't be that difficult, would it?

Step 3: Made a decision to turn our will and lives over to the care of God as we understood Him. The problem is we kind of think we are God. Or we think we are equal to God. Or least we think we are as wise and powerful as God because we are determined to maintain control of our own lives. I'm not sure how many times I have told God exactly how my life should turn out, exactly what I need, and exactly when I need it. But like the demoniac in Luke's Gospel, there comes a point in our lives when we simply throw ourselves at the feet of Jesus and ask, "What have you to do with me, Jesus, Son of the Most High God?" That moment for the demoniac, or for me or you is Step 3. We make a decision to turn our will and our lives over to the care of God as we understand God.

In AA, we start to make that decision as soon as we step through the door for the first time. It's just a start. And once I turned my will and life over to the care of God, then the really difficult task came and that was to also turn everyone else's life over to the care of God. Here is the truth—it really wasn't that hard for me to finally say, "Okay God, here is my life. Take it and do with it whatever you want to do." It was harder to do that with other people because I often still find myself trying to direct their lives—wanting them to believe a certain way, to behave a certain way, or journey a certain way. To be quite honest, we pastors often fall into that kind of thinking because parishioners pull us into it when they seem to say, "Just tell us what to do. Be responsible for our lives, our decisions, and our journeys." I can't do that. I have to turn their lives over to God just as I had to turn my life over to God. Why? Simply because I'm not God and I know that.

On the last night of a revival in Hawkinsville, Georgia, I told the congregation that we were going to have a question and answer time. I told them that they could ask me anything about the sermons I had preached that week or that we could dialogue about anything else that interested them. I know this is kind of risky, but I wanted to know the people and I wanted them to know me. A lot of wonderful things could come out of that kind of dialog. The first question was spoken by a 28-year-old parent who asked, "If you could parent all over again what would you do differently?" I answered quickly, "I would have turned my children over to God a lot sooner." As a parent, I wanted to write their stories. I wanted them to go where I wanted them to go. I wanted them to do what I wanted them to do. I wanted them to be what I wanted them to be. I wanted them to avoid what I wanted them to avoid. That is what I thought good dads do. But here's the deal: even if God had let me write their stories, I would have gotten them wrong because I did not and do not know God's plans for my children's lives. I don't know what they need to endure or what they need to experience to be the people that God wants them to be and to accomplish the tasks that God needs them to accomplish in this world.

Even if God let me write my parishioners' stories, I would get them wrong, because I'm not God. When the demoniac saw Jesus in verse 28, he fell down before Him and shouted at the top of his voice, "What have you to do with me, Jesus, Son of the Most High God?" *What are you going to do with me?* In the very simplest of ways this man was acknowledging Jesus' lordship and control. That acknowledgment is a crucial step for all of us who are looking for some sort of sanity and serenity in our lives. I don't know everything about God, but I know I'm not God.

Another thing I think I know about God is that God operates out of love.

At the annual General Assembly meeting of the Cooperative Baptist Fellowship in Charlotte, North Carolina, I presented an interpretation of the biblical theme for the week based on 1 John 3:1-3. In preparation for the sermon, I read those verses over and over again for several months and came to love the first line of that passage. It says, "See what love the Father has lavished upon us." The biblical witness is that God operates out of love. But we don't always believe and trust this, and sometimes we are even a bit suspicious when it comes to God.

A *Good Housekeeping* survey taken about twelve years ago asked, "Who do you trust the most?" 40% of the people trusted Walter

Cronkite, 26% of the people trusted Pope John Paul, and 12% trusted Billy Graham. God got 3%. We are a little suspicious about God's care. The demoniac came and threw himself at the feet of Jesus and surrendered his life and will to Jesus, but the very next words out of his mouth in verse 29 were, "But do not torment me." We can be a bit suspicious when it comes to God's care. We're not always certain or convinced that God is working in our best interests. Even the people from the demoniac's hometown who heard what happened, and came out to see it, weren't really convinced. Jesus had caused all those demons to go into their swine and then they all went off the cliff to kill themselves. These townspeople looked and found that Jesus had destroyed their livelihood by pulling the whole economic base of their town out from under them. So in verse 37, they asked Jesus to leave town. They didn't trust that he cared.

I'm not saying that God won't disrupt our lives. I'm simply saying that if we surrender our will and our lives to God, God will always care for us. I'm not saying that God causes everything that happens to us. I'm not blaming God for everything. But I am claiming that God walks with us and cares for us in every chapter of our lives. I know that God operates out of love.

Recently I was sharing with a good friend how my view of God has changed and evolved over the years. I used to believe in my heart of hearts and brain of brains, that God was waiting to whack me on the back of my head. You do something wrong, and God is ready to whack you on the back on the head. You get lazy and miss your prayers or your quiet time, and God is waiting to whack you on the back of the head. If things are going really well for a long time in your life, you'd better watch out because God is waiting to whack you on the back of your head and bring you back down. Am I the only one who deals with a "God is waiting to whack you on the back of the head" theology? It has taken a lot of prayer and a lot of living for me to believe in God's care.

How did Jesus say it to his disciples? "When your children ask for bread, you don't give them rocks. When they ask for fish, you don't hand them snakes. If your earthly fathers can give good gifts to their children, how much more will your heavenly Father give to you what is good?" How did John write it? "See what love the Father has lavished upon us." How does Step 3 say it? "Made a decision to turn our will and our lives over to the care of God." The care of God.

I'm thankful for some people's confidence in me, but honestly, I don't know everything about God. What I do know is fairly simple. I'm not God. I can't control or fix my life. I can't control or fix your life. God is not waiting to whack us on the back of the head. The God we worship is waiting with open arms to lavish his love upon us because that is how God operates. We are invited to turn our wills and our lives over to a caring God.

HELPING THE HOARDERS
Galatians 5:1-26

STEP 4

Made a searching and fearless moral inventory of ourselves.

For freedom Christ has set us free. Stand firm, therefore, and do not submit again to a yoke of slavery.

Listen! I, Paul, am telling you that if you let yourselves be circumcised, Christ will be of no benefit to you. Once again I testify to every man who lets himself be circumcised that he is obliged to obey the entire law. You who want to be justified by the law have cut yourselves off from Christ; you have fallen away from grace. For through the Spirit, by faith, we eagerly wait for the hope of righteousness. For in Christ Jesus neither circumcision nor uncircumcision counts for anything; the only thing that counts is faith working through love.

You were running well; who prevented you from obeying the truth? Such persuasion does not come from the one who calls you. A little yeast leavens the whole batch of dough. I am confident about you in the Lord that you will not think otherwise. But whoever it is that is confusing you will pay the penalty. But my friends, why am I still being persecuted if I am still preaching circumcision? In that case the offence of the cross has been removed. I wish those who unsettle you would castrate themselves!

For you were called to freedom, brothers and sisters; only do not use your freedom as an opportunity for self-indulgence, but through love become slaves to one another. For the whole law is summed up in a single commandment, 'You shall love your neighbour as yourself.' If, however, you bite and devour one another, take care that you are not consumed by one another.

Live by the Spirit, I say, and do not gratify the desires of the flesh. For what the flesh desires is opposed to the Spirit, and what the Spirit desires is opposed to the flesh; for these are opposed to each other, to prevent you from doing what you want. But if you are led by the Spirit, you are not subject to the law. Now the works of the flesh are obvious: fornication, impurity, licentiousness, idolatry, sorcery, enmities, strife, jealousy, anger, quarrels, dissensions, factions, envy, drunkenness, carousing, and things like these. I am warning you, as I warned you before: those who do such things will not inherit the kingdom of God.

By contrast, the fruit of the Spirit is love, joy, peace, patience, kindness, generosity, faithfulness, gentleness, and self-control. There is no law against such things. And those who belong to Christ Jesus have crucified the flesh with its passions and desires. If we live by the Spirit, let us also be guided by the Spirit. Let us not become conceited, competing against one another, envying one another.

There is a reality television show called "Hoarders" that just started this season. I'm not sure how I feel about these types of programs. Turning someone else's psychological illness into entertainment is not something that's comfortable for me. However, if the experience helps someone to understand and find help for his or her problem, then that is a good thing. The reality of hoarders is that they tend to save and store everything. They cannot throw anything away. They pile stuff up without sifting through it, inventorying it, or deciding what they should keep and what they need to discard. They never do these things. Some of them never even acknowledge that the hoard is there. Even when most of us can't get rid of some things we at least know that it is there!

Step 4: Made a searching and fearless moral inventory of ourselves. For me, Step 4 is not so much a call to confession as it is a call to being honest about seeing what is there—what you can keep, what you can discard, and what is just going to be there. I love the ending of today's scripture that says two powers are constantly at war with each other. There are things about ourselves that we cannot discard and that we simply have to acknowledge exist. We need to see what is in our life, what we have tucked away, and what we have overlooked. These things affect our behavior and affect our peace and serenity, whether we are consciously or subconsciously tucking them away.

In Galatians 5, Paul talks to us about this discipline of making a fearless and searching moral inventory. He doesn't call it that, but that is exactly what it is. In fact, you will find some wonderful truths in the verses of Galatians 5 that include a listing of the sins that the flesh pushes us toward and a listing of all the truths that the Spirit guides us toward. The first thing that emerges is that we are not perfect people. Well, first, we already know this because we live with ourselves, right? And second, we live with other folks. We know we are not perfect people. We've heard this truth in scripture throughout our lives. Romans 3:23 is a verse that we all learned as children. It says, "For all have sinned and fall short of the glory of God." **We are not perfect.**

The prophet Isaiah tells us that even in our righteousness, the best that we can do looks like filthy rags in the eyes of God. We are not perfect people. When the adulterous woman was brought and thrown before Jesus, and he heard the crowd of accusatory religious people, he said, "The one of you who is without sin, you throw the first rock." Everyone walked away because we know we are not perfect people. Making a searching and fearless moral inventory of our lives helps us come to grips and come face to face with all of these things.

So we read in verses 19, 20, and 21, "Now the works of the flesh are obvious: fornication, impurity, licentiousness, idolatry, sorcery, enmities, strife, jealousy, anger, quarrels, dissensions, factions, envy, drunkenness, carousing, and things like these." When we read those verses, we catch a glimpse of ourselves. You may say, "I don't see myself." But there are other lists of sins I could read and you could find yourself in those lists. If you can't find yourself anywhere in there, maybe self-righteousness is your problem! All of us live with some sort of sin. We aren't perfect. I love the story about the businessman from New England who wrote Mark Twain a letter and said, "Before I die I want to go to the Holy Land, climb Mount Sinai, and scream out to the world the Ten Commandments." Mark Twain, with his brilliant wit and his unique way, wrote a note back to his friend and said, "Wouldn't it be better if you stayed in Boston and kept them yourself?"

Step 4: Made a searching and fearless moral inventory of ourselves. It is not hard to see our own imperfections. But that is just part of doing an inventory of our lives. As I said earlier, I don't want this to digress into some sort of confession. Step 4 is an honest inventory of who we are and the realization that we are not perfect. But when I read this text, I also hear that we are not worthless.

In Genesis 1, after every step of God's creation of the world, God says, "This is good." When God creates humankind, the text says in Hebrew, "This is *very good*." **We are not worthless.** The Psalmist says we are treasured. We know these scriptures and yet we spend a lifetime allowing the world to scream at us, "You are worthless!" The world's voice has gotten so loud and obnoxious that we hear it over and over again and can't seem to get it out of our minds. The world says that you are ugly and you are worthless and you are nobody until you prove you are worth something, until you succeed in something, and earn your way into the good graces of God and the good graces of the people. You have to do something that is relevant, something spectacular, something that is wonderful in your life, or you can't be loved. The world is so loud that it has just about drowned out the voice of God.

It is the voice of God that Jesus heard at his baptism. It's an interesting story. Jesus came up out of the baptismal waters and a voice from the heavens was heard, saying, "This is my beloved child, in whom I am well pleased." Jesus heard it, but everybody standing around said, "It must have been thunder." It is hard for us to hear that we are beloved, worthy children, whom God is absolutely pleased to have as his own.

Another author once wrote, "If God had a refrigerator, every one of your pictures would be on it." As I told a group of people in North Carolina one week, "You are beloved. When I baptize people in the baptistery, I put them under water, I pull them up, and the first words I say to them are, "You are God's beloved child in whom he is well pleased." The world has screamed at us and we have gotten so wrapped up with insecurities, flaws, faults, and defects that we forget who we are. **We are God's beloved.**

Prayer can help us to know this truth. Part of prayer is speaking and part of prayer is listening. In prayer we are invited to speak to and share with God all of the flaws and insecurities that we can conjure in our minds with regard to our lives. In prayer we are invited to listen for the words of God as only God can speak them.

In 1994, legendary country singer, Johnny Cash released an album titled, American Recording. The album cover was in black and white, he was dressed in black and white, and he had a black and white dog standing on each side of him. When someone asked him about the cover's significance, he said, "It just means that I'm not all good and I'm not all bad. I'm just a mix of both. I'm a human being."

Did you hear verses 14 and 15 say that the whole law can be summed up like this: "Love your neighbor as yourself. But if, however, you continue to devour one another you will consume each other."? I find it interesting that I have the capacity to be either a predator or a provider. I think it is interesting that the text says it is our inclination to devour each other but the Spirit guides us to produce fruits of the spirit. We can be predators who prey on each other, living life to tear each other down, to tear life down, and move toward death, or we can be providers who surrender to the Spirit, share the fruits of the spirit in our life and feed each other.

One year when I was in Charlotte for the Cooperative Baptist Fellowship's General Assembly, I went out to eat with several friends. We went to get some ice cream and found ourselves standing in a long line. In front of us was a woman with a little six-year-old boy who was ready for some ice cream. He was jumping up and down, running in and out of line and going over and under the ropes while his mother kept telling him to behave and stay still. When he finally got to the counter, he said that he wanted strawberry ice cream with gummy bears on top. At this point, he was so excited that he could not stand still. Finally, he put his hands up and the server gave him the ice cream; and it was like a gift from heaven. He grabbed it and pulled it down and dug in and got it all over his face. Not knowing what to do next, he turned around and looked at me and said, "Mister do you want a bite?" My friends just looked at me because they knew that I NEVER eat off other people's spoons. I rubbed him on the head and said, "No, but thank you for the offer," and then he went happily skipping, bouncing and moving out the door.

We all took our ice cream and walked out, talking about the little boy. I turned to one of my friends and said, "You know, I wish I had taken that bite." I don't know what that would have done for him, but I know what it would have done for me. Wrapped up in that child was all of the greed and desire that the flesh can hold. But also, wrapped up in that child were the fruits of the spirit. When he was blessed with the greatest blessing ever imagined, he immediately wanted to share it with someone else.

We are not perfect, we are not worthless, and when we make a searching, fearless, moral inventory of our lives, we find that we are simply human, a mix of bad *and* good. We have the ability to be predators or providers and to surrender to the Spirit so that we might live with that kind of tension...as God's beloved children.

WHAT I LIKE ABOUT THE RCC
James 5:13-20

STEP 5

Admitted to God, to ourselves, and to another human being the exact nature of our wrongs.

Are any among you suffering? They should pray. Are any cheerful? They should sing songs of praise. Are any among you sick? They should call for the elders of the church and have them pray over them, anointing them with oil in the name of the Lord. The prayer of faith will save the sick, and the Lord will raise them up; and anyone who has committed sins will be forgiven. Therefore confess your sins to one another, and pray for one another, so that you may be healed. The prayer of the righteous is powerful and effective. Elijah was a human being like us, and he prayed fervently that it might not rain, and for three years and six months it did not rain on the earth. Then he prayed again, and the heaven gave rain and the earth yielded its harvest.

My brothers and sisters, if anyone among you wanders from the truth and is brought back by another, you should know that whoever brings back a sinner from wandering will save the sinner's soul from death and will cover a multitude of sins.

Recently, while attending a conference, I checked into my hotel, went up to my room and opened the window. Straight ahead of me was the convention center. The NASCAR Hall of Fame was to my right, and a Roman Catholic Church was to my left, two blocks away. So the next day around noon, like the good apostate, former Roman Catholic that I am, I decided to skip lunch and walk the two blocks to the church to see if they were having services. The St. Peter's Catholic Church front door was open and there was a sign that said: Mass at 12:15. Just in time! I walked in and sat down on one of the pews. Against the south wall there was a line of people waiting for the confessional booth that was at the back of the sanctuary. All confessions were completed around 12:10. The priest came out at 12:15 and I worshipped with my Roman Catholic brothers and sisters.

I left and went back to the conference for the afternoon activities. As I walked those two blocks again, I realized that there are some things that I really like about the RCC (Roman Catholic Church). For instance, I like that the doors are always open. Most churches are all locked up because we have security concerns. The RCC tends to stay open throughout the day. This is an encouragement for people to come in, sit and spend time with God, pray with other persons, or pray by themselves. I also like it that the RCC worships every day. Sometimes worship services are offered two or three times a day—morning prayers at 7:00 a.m., and mass at 12:15 p.m. Then there is always a big celebration on Sundays, the Lord's Day, with lots of people present. Every day is a day that is set aside for worship and I like that.

I must admit that I like confession too. Step 5 fits right in here. "Admitted to God, to ourselves, and to another human being the exact nature of our wrongs." Every time I think about Step 5, I think about James 5. James says, "Anyone who has committed sins will be forgiven. Therefore, confess your sins to one another, and pray for one another, so that you may be healed." The text doesn't say to confess your sins to yourself or to God, but to confess them to one another so that you might experience the healing that follows. The RCC's open doors invite faithful catholics to that possibility every day.

We don't talk about confession much in the baptist church and maybe we should. It is kind of a shame that when the Protestants left the Roman Catholic tradition, we tended to throw that baby out with the holy bath water. We Baptists have a strong image of the priesthood of the believer. We believe that we don't have to confess our sins to any other human being because we have a direct route to God. And yes we can and do communicate directly with God. But confession to one another also has a place in Christian practice. Scripture often speaks of this kind of confession and I believe that most individuals yearn for it. Here's why: **There is healing for the one who confesses.** There is a sense of healing that happens in us when we confess to another human being. That's why James writes, "Confess your sins to one another so you may experience or know healing."

I have a pastor friend who knows that I have been preaching the Twelve Steps this summer. He sent me an insightful email that said, "Here are some things that you need to share about confession. I hope you tell your congregation that confession heals the soul. It allows us to be fully human, be real before others, and get beyond our presented self." We tend to live our lives with a deliberate self that we present to other people—what we want them to see, and how we want them to know us. But, in the act of confession to another human being, we get to move beyond that presentation and be who we truly are. The second thing he said was, "Confession allows us to let go of the sins that enslave us, sins that we almost worship, and that our lives revolve around." **Confession allows us to be fully human and real, getting beyond our presented self. Confession allows us to let go of sins that enslave us that we almost worship because our lives revolve around them.**

My grandmother was the most saintly woman I have ever known. She never attended church the whole time I knew her, but she had Billy Graham's book collection in her living room, and she watched him on TV religiously. I didn't understand why my grandmother was like this, but that's who she was. My grandmother loved gardening and she had a Bird of Paradise bush in her yard in Arkansas that she loved. One day, my siblings and I were playing chase when I fell into the Bird of Paradise bush and broke off two of the largest, blooming limbs. My sister came over, looked at me lying there with tears in my eyes, and said she was going to tell. I told her, "Please don't tell, I will do anything" to which my sister replied, "You will do anything I tell you?" And I said, "I'll do anything you tell me."

We came in for lunch and our grandmother asked my sister to put the dishes in the dishwasher. My sister leaned over and said, "I think Jimmy is going to do that." I looked at my sister and wondered why in the world I would want to take care of the dishes. My sister whispered, "The Bird of Paradise." "Okay, I'll do it."

In the middle of the afternoon, my grandmother told my sister to take out the trash. She said, "I think Jimmy will do that." I said, "Why would I do that?" Of course. The Bird of Paradise.

Eventually I got so tired of doing all of my sister's chores that I just went to my grandmother and said that I had something to tell her. With tears in my eyes, I said, "We were playing chase today and I fell over while we were running and I fell in your Bird of Paradise bush and I broke off the two biggest limbs. I am really sorry!" That's when my grandmother said, "Jimmy, I already knew you did that. I was looking out the window the whole time and saw you do it." Oh. "Really?" Then she said, "Yes, I was just trying to figure out how long you were going to let your sister ruin your life over it. How long were you going to let it enslave you?"

Many years later, when I was in seminary in Kentucky, my wise and loving grandmother was diagnosed with cancer. When my wife and I got the call that she only had a few days left to live, we loaded up the car and drove to Mississippi. The whole family had gathered because my grandmother was truly loved. At one point, as we were all gathered in the hospital room, she looked up and said that she needed everyone to leave the room but me. I had no idea why I was being asked to stay in the room. I wasn't sure what she wanted. When we

were alone, she said, "Before I die, I need to make a confession to you."
I told my grandmother that she was a saint. But she said, "You listen
to me. Before I die, I need to confess to you." As a twenty-something-
year-old seminary student who worshiped his grandmother, I had to
hear the darkest secret of her life. I tried my best to assure her that she
was forgiven, and then I thought to myself, "That is why she didn't go
to church. That's how she knew that a sin could enslave you for your
whole life until you confess." I just wish she had laid her turmoil and
torment down earlier. Truth be known, that moment with my grandmother made me a more graceful seminary student and pastor, which
is the other great value of the act of confession. **We not only confess
because it somehow heals the one who is doing the confessing.
Confession also heals the one who hears the confession when it is
shared human to human—not me to God, not me to self, but me to
you. It doesn't just heal you to tell me, it heals me to hear you.** Step
5 involves at least two people—one who is sharing the nature of his or
her wrong, and a trusted individual who is listening to the confession.
Both experience healing.

There is a story recorded in chapter 20 of John's gospel where
Jesus comes into the room after his resurrection and says to his disciples, "Peace be with you." Many of us have heard it multiple times,
perhaps enough to wonder why we have to hear it over and over from
the pulpit during the church year. A text about peace and forgiveness.

There was a seminary student who had graduated and
was hired at a church. When he went to preach his trial sermon, he
preached on repentance. It was such a good sermon that he was hired.
The first Sunday that he was there he preached on repentance. On the
second Sunday he preached on repentance, and then on the third Sunday he preached on repentance again. So the deacons started talking
about it and decided to ask him what was going on. "When are you
going to stop preaching the same sermon on repentance?" they asked.
To which he responded, "I guess when you repent."

I'm not sure why this text about peace and forgiveness keeps popping up in our worship. Maybe we just need to hear it a lot. Maybe we need to hear that the sins we forgive are forgiven and the sins we retain are retained. When we hear someone confess his or her sins, what we forgive is forgiven and what we retain is retained. The last time I preached from this text, I encouraged people to be forgivers. One of my parishioners went out the door, shook my hand, and said, "You spent the whole sermon talking about forgiveness and forgiving sins and never said a word about retaining sins." I looked him in the eye and quickly said, "Because we already know how to do that." We already know how to retain other people sins. We are experts in holding things against people, holding grudges, and withholding grace. It is forgiveness that we need to work on and it is the forgiveness that heals.

How long will we be enslaved by our sins? How long will we whisper in others' ears, "Bird of Paradise." It has been said well and often that it is our secrets that keep us sick. The most accurate and best path to sobriety, or serenity, has been proven by thousands of people in the world. Embrace the practice of confession. Admit to God, to yourself, and to another human being the exact nature of your wrongs. As James said, "Your sins will be forgiven." So let's confess our sins to each other and pray for each other. There is healing to be experienced there.

I hope there is someone in your life that you can confess to—a trusted friend, a spiritual director, a therapist, a priest, or a minister. I don't care who it is, just somebody with whom you can lay everything you have ever done and everything you are on a table before them and know the healing that comes from that kind of confession.

CLOSE ENOUGH?

Amos 7:7-17

STEP 6

Were entirely ready to have God remove all these defects of
character.

*This is what he showed me: the Lord was standing beside a wall built
with a plumb-line, with a plumb-line in his hand. And the Lord said to
me, 'Amos, what do you see?' And I said, 'A plumb-line.' Then the Lord
said, 'See, I am setting a plumb-line in the midst of my people Israel; I
will never again pass them by; the high places of Isaac shall be made
desolate, and the sanctuaries of Israel shall be laid waste, and I will rise
against the house of Jeroboam with the sword.'*

*Then Amaziah, the priest of Bethel, sent to King Jeroboam of Is-
rael, saying, 'Amos has conspired against you in the very centre of the
house of Israel; the land is not able to bear all his words. For thus Amos
has said, "Jeroboam shall die by the sword, and Israel must go into exile
away from his land."' And Amaziah said to Amos, 'O seer, go, flee away to
the land of Judah, earn your bread there, and prophesy there; but never
again prophesy at Bethel, for it is the king's sanctuary, and it is a temple
of the kingdom.'*

*Then Amos answered Amaziah, 'I am no prophet, nor a proph-
et's son; but I am a herdsman, and a dresser of sycomore trees, and the
Lord took me from following the flock, and the Lord said to me, "Go,
prophesy to my people Israel."*

'Now therefore hear the word of the Lord. You say, "Do not

prophesy against Israel, and do not preach against the house of Isaac."
Therefore, thus says the Lord: "Your wife shall become a prostitute in the
city, and your sons and your daughters shall fall by the sword, and your
land shall be parceled out by line; you yourself shall die in an unclean
land, and Israel shall surely go into exile away from its land." '

A minister said of Step 6, "This is the step that separates the men from
the boys." Up to now, all we have done is a lot of self searching, soul
searching, and mind thinking, but at this point we say to God, "I'm
ready for you to take all my defects of character away from me."

   You never know what skills a person has hidden within their
treasure chest of talents. I'm going to tell you a little known fact about
Jim Dant. I know how to use an acetylene torch and a welder. My dad
was a sawmill worker in a small private sawmill. He and the workers
took care of the business and their own equipment. When I was in the
eighth grade, my dad put my brother and me on a torch and a welder
for the first time to show us how to use them. My brother had this
great idea that we were going to build a go-cart out of scrap metal and
Dad shocked us by letting us do it. He said, "You boys just be careful."
We began our work. I started cutting segments of angle iron to form
the frame, and measuring and cutting some concrete reinforcement
bars that we were going to twist into shape. Doug, my brother, began
welding the frame and axle together with one of the most ridiculous
steering mechanisms that I have ever seen. Our favorite line through
the whole process was, "That is close enough. That is close enough."

   Throughout that morning, my dad kept walking by us every
once in a while, shaking his head, biting his tongue and not saying a
word. Doug and I kept glancing at each other, wishing and hoping that
he would just leave us alone so we could finish our great project. And
that's when I set Doug's pants on fire. I had wanted to try my hand at
the welding because all of the cutting was done. So I put the welding
hood over my head, welded my little line on two pieces of metal, got

them together, and then laid the rod aside. My brother was sitting beside me and the rod hit his pant leg and set it on fire. We screamed and panicked and then we both started laughing.

That's when my dad jumped in, screaming things like, "You boys are going to kill yourselves. You are not being careful with these tools!" Every frustration he had held all morning long just blew out of him. He started ripping and cutting our go-cart apart while we just sat and watched. Then he spent the whole afternoon rebuilding it with his dreaded internal "plumb line." A plumb line is a weight on a string that builders use, with the help of gravity, to ensure accuracy. My dad had a particular standard for how things were to be done and by which all things should be constructed and we weren't close enough. We weren't even near close enough. While Doug and I said, "That is close enough. That is close enough," it was not close enough to be safe or accurate enough for my dad. In fact, we knew that if Dad was going to get involved, every piece was going to be measured, every angle was going to have to be correct, and it would have to be done right, using the dreaded plumb line.

There was a time in Israel's history—very similar to our Civil War—when the kingdom was divided. The northern kingdom was Israel and the southern kingdom was Judah. The southern kingdom included Jerusalem, the temple, the priests, rituals, altars, and everything else necessary to be God's people. The northern kingdom had none of these things, and the people wondered how they were going to worship. So they constructed their own altars, appointed their own priests, and established their own rituals. None of these things were done according to the standards of Torah law but the people just figured it was close enough. For decades, God just kept passing by and passing by and shaking God's head until God couldn't stand it any longer. Then he told Amos, "You go tell those people I'm setting a plumb line in the midst of Israel and I will never pass them by again." I admit that the rest of God's words sound pretty harsh. The high places are going to be made desolate, the sanctuaries are going to be laid waste, the house of Jeroboam is going to know the sword. All of Israel is about to go into exile. It sounds really harsh, but then, you should have seen my dad tear apart that go-cart! We tend to think of plumb lines as something to dread. They are the judgmental eye that leads to painful correction. **But the good news of the gospel is this: God's plumb line, as harsh as it may sound, is a very graceful plumb line.**

Listen to verse 8 again. "I am setting a plumb line in the midst of my people Israel and I will never again pass them by." Perhaps God is saying, "It might be painful for me to stop, but I'm not just passing by anymore." God has been passing by us for centuries. Do you remember that Moses wanted to see the face of God? God said, "No, here is what I will do. I'll stick you in the cleft of a rock and I'll pass by and you can see me pass by, but you can't see my face." David heard a whisper of God in the songs and psalms that entered into his heart. There is an honesty in those psalms when David says, "God is a God who hides His face. He just keeps passing by." Isaiah, one of Israel's greatest prophets, saw smoke and angels in the temple, and felt the very foundations of the temple shake one day, but he never saw God's face. He affirms this in his writings by saying, "God you are truly a God who hides yourself. You just keep passing by."

So God said to Amos, "I'm setting a plumb line in the midst of my people Israel and I will never pass them by again." The opposite of passing by is stopping for a while, dwelling with us, and being with us. It is God with us—Emmanuel. In Christ, God stopped passing us by. In Christ, we believe that God stopped and dwelled with us for a while. We got to see the face of God. We got to see the standard and the plumb line of God. We got to see in Christ what God expects. **What we saw in Christ was what humanity was meant to be and that is nothing to dread.**

Doug and I dreaded our dad stopping and sitting with us, seeing the mess we had made, and correcting our mistakes. But after he ripped our go-cart apart, I wish you could have seen the one he built for us! We played with that go-cart for years.

In Christ, God takes our messes, our worst attempts at life, the consequences of our poorest decisions, all of our defects of character, and puts his graceful plumb line alongside them. He corrects and heals and balances. Yes, sometimes it is a little painful, but it is also a graceful gift. We do not serve a God who sees the struggles and the messes of our lives and then chooses to pass us by. This God is a Good Samaritan. This God is a good Savior whose body was broken and whose blood was shed for our sake.

Several years ago, Bill Gaither wrote a song titled, "Something Beautiful" that includes these words in the chorus:

> Something beautiful, something good, all my confusion, He understood. All I had to offer Him was brokenness and strife, but He made something beautiful of my life.

Our God is a good God who comes and dwells with us, gets in the mess with us, helps, and heals us. He doesn't just pass us by.

A DISTANT SECOND
Luke 10:38-42

STEP 7

Humbly asked Him to remove our shortcomings.

Now as they went on their way, he entered a certain village, where a woman named Martha welcomed him into her home. She had a sister named Mary, who sat at the Lord's feet and listened to what he was saying. But Martha was distracted by her many tasks; so she came to him and asked, 'Lord, do you not care that my sister has left me to do all the work by myself? Tell her then to help me.' But the Lord answered her, 'Martha, Martha, you are worried and distracted by many things; there is need of only one thing. Mary has chosen the better part, which will not be taken away from her.'

Tim Russert was the NBC Washington Bureau Chief and also "Meet the Press" moderator for years and years. Very few journalists ever had a private audience with Pope John II before his death. Tim Russert was one of those journalists. His task was to convince the Pope to appear on "The Today Show." Since he had once served as an altar boy, the show's producers thought he was the perfect person to speak to the pontiff. Tim Russert said that when he walked into the room, he was immediately filled with a sense of holiness. And when he saw the Pope, he blurted out with tears, "Bless me, Father."

Pope John Paul II embraced him, then stepped back, looked

into his face, and said, "You are the one called Timothy, the man from NBC."

Russert said, "Yes, Father."

John Paul II said, "They tell me you are a very important man."

To which Tim Russert responded, "There are only two of us in this room and I am certainly a distant second."

Martha received Christ. There should be no doubt about this. We have all read or heard this story in the context of our Sunday School classes and Bible studies. In verse 38, Jesus enters a certain village and it is Martha who welcomes him into the village and welcomes him into her home. In verse 40, it is Martha who is busy with a multitude of tasks related to making Jesus' stay comfortable. If we read the passage carefully, we see that Martha is the only person who speaks to Jesus in these few verses!

Martha was a woman of action; she had an active faith. She expressed her welcome and her love for Jesus through her actions; that was who she was. She welcomed him with Jewish hospitality. She worked and served him because she apparently understood that 'by our fruits we are known.' She spoke directly to Jesus...sharing her concerns and her complaints...because when there is an issue in the air, you might as well state it, deal with it, and solve it, rather than sit on it. Martha was a woman of action.

I miss Earl Farriba. I was sitting in the living room this week... on the sofa...with my laptop on my lap. I was spending the evening sifting through old files. One of the file folders I came across was labeled—Funeral Sermons. Embedded in the electronic niche were eulogies I had delivered over the last several years. I quietly read the names of people—family and friends—who had passed away. I realized I missed a lot of people. But when I clicked down to Earl's name, I realized I really miss Earl Farriba. He spent a lot time at the church. Every week...almost every day...he was digging trenches and crawling into ceilings and wrestling pipes and ropes and ladders. If I heard it once, I heard it 100 times, 'you can't out work Earl Farriba.' That is the way Earl received and served Christ. That is the way he expressed his love for Christ. That is Martha.

Mary received Christ. Verse 39 says that Martha had a sister named Mary and she came and sat at the Lord's feet; she quietly listened to what he was saying. That was not Martha's way of receiving... but it is still a form of receiving. It looks very familiar, sounds very familiar and feels very familiar to us. It is a posture that is assumed in the presence of a great teacher or a great rabbi; certainly in the presence of Jesus. Over against busyness and service (which was Martha's way of receiving and expressing) this is a love that is expressed through quiet, prayerful attentiveness. It was the way Mary received Christ and expressed her love for Christ.

On the second Tuesday evening of each month, Highland Hills Baptist Church in Macon, Georgia provides a Taize worship service for the congregation and community. It is a wonderful service. As pastor of the congregation, I received numerous compliments with regard to that service. People expressed their love for the music, their connection with the prayers, and their enjoyment of the readings. The most common comment, however, was, "I love the silence." During the service we pause for no less than ten minutes of silence. We sit quietly before God and express our love for God in the privacy of our hearts. We listen and trust God to speak to us.

I was on a pastors' retreat about three years ago. Ministers from all different denominations gathered for the three-day event. As we gathered for one of our afternoon group sessions, the leader of the retreat instructed us, "I want you to spend 30 minutes in silent prayer—just you and God. I don't care where you go, but find a quiet place where you can listen for the voice of God. After 30 minutes, we will re-gather." When the allotted time had passed, we congregated in the assigned space. Well...not all of us. Ron didn't show up. We waited on him for a while, then—having given up on his participation—began our time of sharing without him. When the session ended, we retired to our midafternoon game of poker...followed by supper...and then casual conversation in the lobby of the retreat center. It was here Ron finally showed up!

"Where have you been?" we asked.

He said it was hard to explain. "I began praying—planning to only pray for 30 minutes—but I got so wrapped up in conversation with God...well...the next thing I knew, I looked at my watch, and realized I'd been praying for four hours later!"

The 'Mary's' in our crowd were awed by intensity of his prayer. The 'Martha's' in the room couldn't believe he missed supper AND the poker game!

David is a member of a former church were I pastored. At some point in his adult life, he became interested in puppet ministry. He started buying puppets and buying puppet scripts and buying—even sewing—puppet outfits! He built a puppet stages complete with multiple levels and backdrops. He annually requested the church to include more and more money in the budget for his puppet ministry. One day he came into my office and said that he was a frustrated. "There are just not enough people who are getting involved in the puppet ministry." He said. "We need more money, more puppeteers, and more people supporting us. I think everybody in the church should be interested in puppet ministry."

I paused. And with a very vulnerable look on my face told David, "Uhhh...I'm scared of puppets...and clowns...and those ventriloquist dolls! I wouldn't want to be involved in a puppet ministry! There are probably others just like me. Some people will want to be involved and some people won't."

David thought everyone should serve and appreciate Christ in the same way he did. And therein lies the rub. It's when we are on retreat and someone spends their time praying for four hours...and misses the poker game. It's when those who need the 'fellowship of poker' judge those who need the fellowship of prayer...and vice versa. It happens when someone is genuinely committed to a ministry of the church—a way of being faithful—and can't get everybody else to express faith in the same manner.

Where is the rub between Martha and Mary? It is in the moment of comparison. For us, it is the moment we judge either Martha or Mary's devotion to Jesus to be more valid than the other. When we look at any other person's reception of Jesus or any other person's expression of love for Jesus and say, "you should...must...ought to express your love 'this' way."

The fact is...we receive Christ differently. We come to know Christ in different ways and express our love for Christ in different ways. The problem occurs in this text—and in our lives—when we begin to compare.

We live in a culture of comparison. I'm obsessed, as a lot of you are, with television shows like "Top Chef," "Chopped," and "Project Runway." All of these shows are based upon the comparison of clothing, cooking styles, and people's appearance. Who cooks and dresses 'right' and who cooks and dresses 'wrong.' When we read this text, we want to know who got it right and who got it wrong. Those of us who are busy people want Martha to get it right. And those of us who are lazy people...well, a little more 'type b'...want Mary to get it right. The truth is, deep down, we all want to please God. So we start comparing and therein lies the problem. When we look at others, we lose our own sense of humility.

Step 7, the next step in our series on recovery, says, "Humbly asked God to remove our shortcomings." Humbly means with humility. We asked God to remove our shortcomings, not their shortcomings, or his shortcomings, or her shortcomings, but my shortcomings. When Jesus says that Mary has chosen the better part or the better portion or the better way, I don't think he is referring to the fact that she is sitting and praying while Martha is working. I don't think he means that she is being still and Martha is busy or that she is not busy serving while Martha is doing all the work. It is simply that Mary is not comparing. That is the better way. She is allowing Martha to love in Martha's way and Mary is choosing to love in Mary's way. Both of these ways have their strengths and both of these ways have their short-comings. In fact, we would do well to humbly balance and appreciate both of these approaches in the expressing of our faith.

Let's not make a cartoon out of this. Martha is not up to her eyeballs in soapsuds. Mary is not sitting pensively on a stool hanging onto every scriptural word that flows out of Jesus' mouth while all the dishes pile up in the sink. If we censure Martha too harshly, she might abandon serving. And if we commend Mary too profusely, she might just sit there forever. There is a time to go and do and there is a time to reflect and listen. Knowing which to do when is a matter of spiritual discernment.

I've read this text many times over the years and honestly... naively asked, "Okay, Jesus, which one is the best one—Mary or Martha?" I think I've heard him say, "Yes. Both." Humility reminds me that I am human. Being human sets parameters for how I relate to God. I respond to God in different ways at different times. Sometimes my faith is about doing; but sometimes it is just about being. Humility also defines my relationships with others. With all the Mary's and Martha's of the world, I am on equal ground before God. The only human shortcomings I need to worry about are my own. (I am much better at asking God to remove what I perceive as the shortcomings of others. You know, why isn't Mary helping with the dishes?) It is good for me to be reminded of the words of Civil rights activist Cornel West. He said it this way, "Humility means two things: a capacity for self-awareness and the ability to let others shine, to empower them in an affirming way."

Tim Russert was the NBC Washington Bureau Chief and also "Meet the Press" moderator for years and years. Very few journalists ever had a private audience with Pope John II before his death. Tim Russert was one of those journalists. His task was to convince the Pope to appear on "The Today Show." Since he had once served as an altar boy, the show's producers thought he was the perfect person to speak to the pontiff. Tim Russert said that when he walked into the room, he was immediately filled with a sense of holiness. And when he saw the Pope, he blurted out with tears, "Bless me, Father."

Pope John Paul II embraced him, then stepped back, looked into his face, and said, "You are the one called Timothy, the man from NBC."

Russert said, "Yes, Father."

John Paul II said, "They tell me you are a very important man."

To whichTim Russert responded, "There are only two of us in this room and I am certainly a distant second."

I am wondering what our lives would look like...what the church would look like...if we all chose to be a distant second. Both in our relationship to God and our relationships with the other people we live with and work with and worship with...people who experience Christ and express their love for Christ with us—but in different ways.

WHAT'S IN A NAME?

Hosea 1

STEPS 8 & 9

Made a list of all persons we had harmed, and became willing to make amends to them all.

Made direct amends to such people wherever possible, except when to do so would injure them or others.

The word of the Lord that came to Hosea son of Beeri, in the days of Kings Uzziah, Jotham, Ahaz, and Hezekiah of Judah, and in the days of King Jeroboam son of Joash of Israel. When the Lord first spoke through Hosea, the Lord said to Hosea, 'Go, take for yourself a wife of whoredom and have children of whoredom, for the land commits great whoredom by forsaking the Lord.' So he went and took Gomer daughter of Diblaim, and she conceived and bore him a son. And the Lord said to him, 'Name him Jezreel; for in a little while I will punish the house of Jehu for the blood of Jezreel, and I will put an end to the kingdom of the house of Israel. On that day I will break the bow of Israel in the valley of Jezreel.'

She conceived again and bore a daughter. Then the Lord said to him, 'Name her Lo-ruhamah, for I will no longer have pity on the house of Israel or forgive them. But I will have pity on the house of Judah, and I will save them by the Lord their God; I will not save them by bow, or by sword, or by war, or by horses, or by horsemen.'

When she had weaned Lo-ruhamah, she conceived and bore a son. Then the Lord said, 'Name him Lo-ammi, for you are not my people and I am not your God.'

Yet the number of the people of Israel shall be like the sand of the sea, which can be neither measured nor numbered; and in the place where it was said to them, 'You are not my people', it shall be said to them, 'Children of the living God.' The people of Judah and the people of Israel shall be gathered together, and they shall appoint for themselves one head; and they shall take possession of the land, for great shall be the day of Jezreel.

If you are like me, the mere mention of some names can raise your blood pressure and your tension levels. Just hearing the name will at least raise an eyebrow because the name is filled with so much baggage. Some of these people? We really don't know them...but we have a sense of the immensity of their baggage. I was listening to the news last night and heard three different names: Lindsay Lohan, there's a load of baggage; George Steinbrenner who recently died, all kinds of baggage accompanies that name; and Hitler even made the evening report, where does one begin sifting that baggage.

That is Hosea 1. It may not feel that way to us because we live in a different age and a different day and these names seem old and obscure. But each of the names mentioned in Hosea 1 comes complete with it's on pile of stuff. In verse 1, there is a listing of kings. If we had been a part of the Israelite family, reading this decades and centuries ago, we would quickly recognize each of these names and the stuff that goes with them. There is Uzziah, who went into the temple and performed a false burning of incense. He was struck with leprosy for his misdeed. Every time you heard his name you would think of that. Then there's Ahaz who willingly surrendered to wickedness and eventually sacrificed his own son through the reinstitution of child sacrifices in Israel. His name forever became associated with that incident and era. Hezekiah is next. Hezekiah, who saw that Israel was probably going to fall from its place of historical prominence, decided to do nothing about it. He assumed the collapse wouldn't happen until after his death...so who cares. His name became associated with dropping the future of Israel on the shoulders of his children and grandchildren.

Read on in the chapter and there are more names—the children of Hosea in chapter 4: Jezreel, a valley, which was known for the slaughter of people, Lo-ruhamah, a name that means, "not pity," and Lo-ammi, a name that means, "you are not my people." What do all these names in Hosea mean to us and what in the world do they have to do with Steps 8 and 9?

Naming allows us to state the issue. Lo-ruhamah and Lo-ammi, you are not going to be pitied and you are not my people. Let's just state the issue.

Several years ago, a couple came into my office for counseling. After sitting in silence for a moment, the wife looked at the floor and finally said, "My husband has a gambling problem and it has led to financial problems. Dr. Dant, we need you to keep this confidential because we don't want our children to know and we don't want our parents to know." The first words out of his mouth were, "They probably already know."

There are few family secrets that are really family secrets. We try to keep a lot of our pain and our problems hidden. If we are really honest, we take our pain and problems and generalize them, or rationalize them, or even spiritualize them. But Hosea—and Step 8—tells us to name them because naming allows us to state the issue.

Step 8 encourages us to write the names of those we have harmed because until you name them...until we acknowledge the harm...the behavior cannot be amended. So we name it. It's what we call getting rid of the elephants in the room. There is stuff going on in our families and in our society and in our churches that tempt us to look the other way and talk of other things. But until the issues are named, they cannot be amended or healed.

A family brought their eight-year-old son to the office several years ago because he was struggling in school and several other social settings. I knew his father had died a couple of months before. The family sat in my office and spent fifteen minutes speaking of everything but the death of his father. Finally, I looked the young boy in the eyes and said, "You are hurting because your father died, aren't you?" He just started crying. And it doesn't matter if you are eight or eighty. I recently sat in the home of an elder female parishioner. The family had asked me to sit with them as they spoke to their mother concerning the inevitable limits that accompany the aging process. They spent the better part of an hour trying to talk to their mom about insurance and laws and financial responsibilities. She finally looked up at me and said, "They want to take away my car keys, don't they?" Just name it.

Fifteen years ago, when I became the pastor of Highland Hills Baptist Church in Macon, Georgia. During our first Sunday of worship together, we read a covenant and agreed to allow it to guide our common ministry and fellowship. In part, the covenant instructed the congregation to say, "...the communication between the pastor and the people of this church is vital to the health of this church; therefore, we promise that when we are hurting or mad we will talk with you and expect the same from you. We will express our support for you and the church and for one another publicly and privately. We will be honest in what we hold in our hearts..."

What we said to each other that day was the same thing the book of Hosea said and the same thing that Step 8 expresses—name it. No elephants in the room, no gossip in the hallway, no blood pressure or tensions rising when we hear each other's names. Until we state the issue and deal with it, it burdens us and makes us sick. Of course, naming doesn't just allow us to state the issue. If that was all this chapter contained, we would be left in a negative and hopeless place, wouldn't we? In fact, the first nine verses feel very negative as we listen to the names of the kings, and the names of the children, and God finally says, "You are not my people."

But thankfully, naming doesn't just allow us to state the issue; it also allows us to amend. So in verse 10 there is a shift in the feel of this text. In verse 9 we hear, "You are not my people and I am not your God…" But in verse 10 the mood changes with the words, "Yet the number of the people of Israel shall be like the sand of the sea, which can be neither measured nor numbered; and in the place where it was said to them, 'You are not my people,' it shall be said to them, 'Children of the living God.'" Naming allows us to state the issue and also allows us to amend.

The present condition of our lives does not necessarily dictate what will be. Stating what is doesn't mean we have to stay there. It actually helps us move toward what can be. Once we have named an issue and acknowledged it, we are free to move toward new possibilities and new realities. We can amend our behavior and maybe even mend relationships. In Hosea, those named "not pity" and "not my people" eventually become the beloved and numerous children of God.

Many persons in Alcoholics Anonymous, Al-Anon, and other recovery programs, fear these two steps…avoid these two steps. They will move somewhat comfortably through Step 7 but will stop at Steps 8 and 9. For those who take up the challenge, however, a multitude of miracles are witnessed. **When we name the issues and address the issues, we are tilling fertile soil where God can do God's work.**

I began working Step 8 and 9 a few years ago. I surveyed almost fifty years of my life and made a list of persons that I had harmed from as far back as I could remember. I began making amends directly or by telephone…person by person by person. Of course, the obvious problem was there were some people on that list that I hadn't seen in years—some of them for decades. I put them in another column and figured I'd just pray for them. I would ask God to forgive me and offer an honest and heartfelt prayer for them…because who knows where they were anyway?

The month I made the list, I attended the inaugural New

Baptist Covenant meeting in Atlanta. I don't know how many hundreds or thousands of people attended that meeting. I was sitting at the Mercer University Press booth signing the book I had written that year, "The Truth is Sensational Enough." John Grisham was signing his new book in a booth nearby. The line for his signature was down the hall, around the corner, and back down another hallway. I had two people in my line...so I was spending a lot of time with them. The first person was someone I knew quite well. We chit-chatted a bit, I signed the book and handed it to her. The second person in line was someone on my list; I had not seen him for almost thirty years! And yet, the month I made the list, we cross paths. I signed the book...and then made my amend. I told this friend from years ago, "I am working my way through the Twelve Steps of recovery and your name is on my 'amends list.' I need to apologize for something I did decades ago." It was a freeing moment. It was a miracle to simply find the courage to amend my behavior and apologize for something I had done. It was a greater miracle to see that in one month God pulled into my path someone that I hadn't seen in so long...that I needed to see.

The story only gets better, however. The very next night I attended a dinner where former Vice President Al Gore was scheduled to speak. While finishing dessert and awaiting the speaker, someone came up behind me and tapped me on the shoulder and said, "You are Jim Dant, aren't you?" I turned around...and there was Jay. I had not seen for about 28 years—since my freshman year of college. He was on the list! That's two people in two days from a list that was made in that same month. After reacquainting ourselves, Jay went back to his table. I thought to myself, "If I don't walk over there now and take care of this, I may not see him for another 20 years." So I got up while everyone was finishing their meal. I approached Jay and asked, "Can I walk out in the hall with you and talk for a minute?" We went outside and I apologized for a college prank that went just a little too far. He started laughing and said he had forgotten about the incident years ago. I said, "I hadn't."

Naming allows us to state the issue. It allows us to move beyond what is to what can be. Naming and addressing the issues tills up fertile soil so God can do God's good and miraculous work in our lives. It almost sounds cruel when God says to Hosea, "Name your children 'valley of slaughter,' 'not pity,' and 'not my people.' But as hard as that all sounds, we know that when harm is named, it can be amended.

NOW I LAY ME DOWN TO SLEEP

Luke 12:13-21

STEP 10

Continued to take personal inventory and when we were wrong promptly admitted it.

Someone in the crowd said to him, 'Teacher, tell my brother to divide the family inheritance with me.' But he said to him, 'Friend, who set me to be a judge or arbitrator over you?' And he said to them, 'Take care! Be on your guard against all kinds of greed; for one's life does not consist in the abundance of possessions.' Then he told them a parable: 'The land of a rich man produced abundantly. And he thought to himself, "What should I do, for I have no place to store my crops?" Then he said, "I will do this: I will pull down my barns and build larger ones, and there I will store all my grain and my goods. And I will say to my soul, Soul, you have ample goods laid up for many years; relax, eat, drink, be merry." But God said to him, "You fool! This very night your life is being demanded of you. And the things you have prepared, whose will they be?" So it is with those who store up treasures for themselves but are not rich towards God.'

Step 10: "Continued to take personal inventory and when we were wrong promptly admitted it." This is a step that takes the church back to the early 1500s when St. Ignatius offered some spiritual exercises to Christians. One of those spiritual exercises was the Prayer of Examen. St. Ignatius' Prayer of Examen is quite simple. We look back on the day that has passed and remember those moments that glorified God the most and those moments that glorified God the least. We let God bring to mind the best and worst moments of the day, the moments when we felt the most and least alive. We offer all of them to God and pray:

> "O mighty God, for your guidance in these moments we are thankful and even more for your grace in these moments we are thankful. Remind us again of your forgiveness; remind us of your steadfast love; remind us that you never forsake us and you always walk with us into the next day, challenging us, encouraging us, admonishing us, and shaping us to become the people you called us to be. In Christ's name we pray, Amen."

Step 10: "Continued to take personal inventory and when we were wrong promptly admitted it." Nighttime prayers used to be very easy for me. In the earliest days it was, "Now I lay me down to sleep" and I could quickly turn over in bed and go to sleep. Later on, my grandmother started praying with me because she was concerned that I wasn't truly talking with God. She would kneel down beside me and say, "Have you told God everything that you are thankful for?" You know the kind of prayer that goes "I'm thankful for the trees and the birds and the dogs and the cats and everything." I would then pray for everybody I wanted God to watch over. I prayed for mom, dad, grandma, granddad, my brothers and sisters. Those were pretty easy prayers. Nighttime prayers get a little harder as you get a little older and become a little more self-aware.

Little Tommy was in Sunday School class when they were trying to teach the children about confession. The teacher had a wonderful idea. She asked all the children to write down everything that they had done wrong the prior week, take the list home, pray with their parents that night and ask God to forgive them. So when Tommy got home that night he knelt down by the bed with his mom and closed his eyes and said, "Dear God, I'm sorry I stole the comic book this week from the drugstore. I'm sorry for all those cuss words I said. I'm sorry I tried that cigarette, and I'm sorry I beat up Billy down the street." His mother was just aghast! Finally when Tommy said, "Amen," she turned him toward her and asked, "When did you do all this stuff?" "Mom, this isn't my list," Tommy said, "This is Mark's. But he knew if he took it home and prayed it tonight, he would get in trouble, so I took it for him." It is difficult to examine ourselves. It is hard to have an objective eye, and at the same time a merciful and honest eye when we inventory our own lives. It is always tempting to be too easy on ourselves or too full of ourselves or too hard on ourselves.

I faithfully have an annual physical. I'm not going to share with you everything the doctor said during my last visit, but he looked over my chart, looked at me and the first words out of his mouth were, "You are slipping." Well, that is encouraging, isn't it? After he went through this whole course of things that were "slipping" in my life from blood pressure to heart rate, he finally said, "You know, you have spent a lot of time in the sun during your lifetime, particularly with all your running. You need to go see a dermatologist." He wrote me one of those go-see-a-dermatologist sheets of paper and I got home and thought to myself, "Surely I can look in the mirror and do this myself, right? I've got a mole here on my shoulder that has been here a long time and it's okay. There's a spot here under my neck that is from running in the sun and I'm sure it will be gone when winter comes. And on my shoulder I've got this little place that is kind of rashy, but that is just from my t-shirt rubbing against it. Looking in the mirror, I don't look that bad for an almost 50-year-old man." If a dermatological assessment was left up to me, I would go easy on myself.

The rich man in Jesus' parable was a little full of himself. That's the way it is sometimes when we do self-examinations. In verse 16, it says that the land had brought forth plenty. It was God's land that had pushed the wheat and the grain up, but if you listen closely to verses 17 and 19, this rich man uses the work "I" eleven times! "I look at my fields and at what I did, and I've got so much now that I think I'm going to store it up, but my barns aren't big enough. So I'll build bigger barns and I'm going to say to my soul that I am doing really good here. Relax and eat and drink and be merry." Nowhere in his examination of life do we see God's hands or does he allow God's eyes to look. **Examining ourselves is difficult. It can lead us to be full of ourselves or easy on ourselves.**

"The Twelve Steps and Twelve Traditions of Alcoholics Anonymous," which is a guidebook for AA participants, very astutely observes this: If temperamentally you lean to the depressive side, self-examination will lead you to guilt and if temperamentally you lean to the self-righteous side, you are going to quickly rationalize every behavior in your life. In other words, it is hard to have an honest, objective, merciful, humble prospective when we look at ourselves. **We tend to be prone to self-abuse or self-righteousness and that is why we do an examination with God.**

The Prayer of Examen is not a prayer we do by ourselves just to reflect on the day. It is a prayer we share with God. The Twelve Steps were written in the early 1900s, but the practice of self-examination is not new. Four hundred years prior, St. Ignatius said that one of the first spiritual disciplines is the Prayer of Examen. But we do it with God. We allow God to lead us into the day that has been lived and it is the eyes, mercy and challenge of God that we follow. God participates in our self-examination.

Actually this practice is really older than the sixteenth century, isn't it? One day Moses was chitchatting with a burning bush and God told him, "You are to go to Egypt and deliver the people of Israel." And Moses said, "I've looked at myself and there is no way I can do this. I'm not a leader. I'm not a speaker. They are not going to respect me." And God said, "I've looked at you and here is what I see."

The temple shook in Isaiah 6, and Isaiah came before the Lord and said, "I can't do anything for you. I am a man of unclean lips." God looked at Isaiah and said, "Here is what I see when I look at you." In Jeremiah 1, God called Jeremiah to speak to the children of Israel and Jeremiah said, "I'm just a boy, I can't speak." God said, "Don't call yourself a boy. I will tell you what to say when I anoint you."

The merciful, challenging, understanding eyes of God see us for who we are—at our best and at our worst. **God wants a say in our examination.** God doesn't want us to look at our lives and condemn ourselves for what we have done or what we haven't done. God wants a say in our examination. That is why we pray for the grace to allow God to guide us through the review of our days.

Usually when I have heard this story read or preached on, the preacher usually ends by saying, "See there, that is what you get for having lots of possessions. That is what you get for being rich and storing stuff up in barns. God will pop you dead if you do those sorts of things. That is what you get." But that is not the way the story ends. The story ends in verses 20 and 21 by saying, "You fool, this very night your life is going to be demanded of you and all the things you have prepared—whose are they going to be?" Here is the moral of the story: "So it is with those who store up treasures for themselves, but are not rich toward God." There are those who have, but don't let God have a say in their life. His sin was not letting God participate in Examen.

I imagine that if this rich farmer, who had stored up grain in multiple barns, had laid down that night and said, "God, you know the good thing is that I have way more than I know what to do with, but the bad thing is that I don't know what to do with it. I need some guidance," God might not have called him a fool. God might have said, "You are fine. There is nothing wrong with what you have and what you have stored. Thank you for letting me have a say in what happens at the end of this day. Here is what we need to do together with the life and the wealth that you have."

Step 10 is not some self-examination where we either rationalize who we are or give up who we are. Step 10 is when we lie down
at night and say, "God, this is who I am. What did I do well today and
what did I not do so well and what can we do together tomorrow?"
It is an examination with God. A self-examine without God has way
too many pitfalls. I wonder what we would look like, what the church
would look like, what we would be doing, and who we would be if we
allowed God that kind of access to the examination of our lives. "God,
this is who I am—the best and the worst of me. Now, what do we need
to do tomorrow?"

In his early 50s, Dennis Lewis was a very successful CEO in a
mid-size company but was feeling out of sorts. He was going through
that whole thought process of wondering, "Is this all there is to life? Is
this everything I'm going to do? Is this my purpose in life?" He decided
to see a therapist who told him that it sounded like he was in a mid-
life crisis. Every question he was asking sounded typical, but Dennis
decided to follow up and see his minister as well. He was not satisfied
that this was just a mid-life crisis. His minister listened to his story, his
questions and the therapist's words and finally said to him, "I think
you are having a spiritual crisis and not a mid-life crisis. Here is what I
suggest you do. I suggest you go home and do a final prayer of examen.
It is an interesting practice that comes out of St. Ignatius' tradition.
Go home, lie down tonight and picture yourself as a 95-year-old man
on the day before you die. Look back and ask yourself what you are
most grateful for and what you are the least grateful for. Ask what God
might have led you to do differently." As a result of that examination,
today Dennis is a drug rehab counselor and a writer. He spends most
of his free time gardening and fishing with his aging father.

I wonder what we would look like, what the church would look
like, what we would be doing, and who we would be, if we allowed God
that kind of access into the examination of our lives.

Prayer in Many Forms

Isaiah 1:10-20

Step 11

Sought through prayer and meditation to improve our conscious contact with God, as we understood Him, praying only for knowledge of His will for us and the power to carry that out.

Hear the word of the Lord, you rulers of Sodom! Listen to the teaching of our God you people of Gomorrah! What to me is the multitude of your sacrifices? says the Lord; I have had enough of burnt-offerings of rams and the fat of fed beasts; I do not delight in the blood of bulls, or of lambs, or of goats.

When you come to appear before me, who asked this from your hand? Trample my courts no more; bringing offerings is futile; incense is an abomination to me. New moon and sabbath and calling of convocation— I cannot endure solemn assemblies with iniquity. Your new moons and your appointed festivals my soul hates; they have become a burden to me, I am weary of bearing them.

When you stretch out your hands, I will hide my eyes from you; even though you make many prayers, I will not listen; your hands are full of blood. Wash yourselves; make yourselves clean; remove the evil of your doings from before my eyes; cease to do evil, learn to do good; seek justice, rescue the oppressed, defend the orphan, plead for the widow.

Come now, let us argue it out, says the Lord: though your sins are like scarlet, they shall be like snow; though they are red like crimson, they shall become like wool. If you are willing and obedient, you shall

eat the good of the land; but if you refuse and rebel, you shall be de-
voured by the sword; for the mouth of the Lord has spoken.

When I was in the high school youth group we used to sing a chorus called, "Come Let Us Reason." It went like this: "Come, let us reason together, that's what God says, come, let us reason together, says the Lord."

The song was a gentle chorus we used to call us to worship. It made us feel good about being in God's presence. "Come, let us reason together says the Lord." These words are based on Isaiah 1:18, but this is not the best translation of the verse. The Hebrew actually says "Let us argue it out." That wonderful, calm chorus of my younger days doesn't come close to touching the emotion that I hear in this text. It's as if God is saying, "This is what you people are doing and I'm tired of it. You come stand before me and let us argue this out." God is inciting an argument in this text. In fact, God begins in verse 10 by calling us "rulers of Sodom" and "people of Gomorrah." What is that all about? "Come let us argue this out. Come before me and let's argue this out." Alright, God.

Here's my argument. "Okay, God, I will argue this out with you. First of all, stop the name-calling. I know sometimes you get angry because we sing praises in worship and we don't mean them. We withhold our gifts from you, and we say prayers off the top of our head without thinking about what we are saying. We hear your word preached and we don't assimilate it into our lives. We hear your laws and we ignore them. We see the needs in your world and we don't meet them. I know at times we anger you—but Sodom and Gomorrah? Come on! You said you would have saved Sodom and Gomorrah if there had been ten righteous folk in the two cities and there are more than ten righteous people in my church today. I'm sure that there are at least eleven! God, I much prefer it when you call us your 'beloved,' your 'children,' like you do at our baptisms. Calling us these names doesn't help a bit. Calling us rulers and people of Sodom and Gomorrah! I promise you this, God: I will not take your name in vain, but please remember mine. I am your child and you are my Father. So if we are going to argue, we have to stop the name-calling, because that is no way to argue."

"And God, if you really want to argue, here goes: In verse 12, you asked the question, "Who demanded all these sacrifices and offerings from you?" In verse 14, you mentioned our new moons and our festivals. Allow me to set the record straight. All that stuff is your stuff. You are the one who asked for this stuff from our hands. In the first seven chapters of Leviticus, you demanded a whole list of sacrifices and offerings—grain offerings, peace offerings, sin offerings, guilt offerings, and burnt offerings. You told us to teach this perpetually to every generation—not just the next generation, not just ten generations, and not just until Jesus came. You told us to teach this perpetually to every generation. And, tucked in those seven chapters, you gave detailed instructions about how each one of these offerings was to be presented to you, or else! This is your stuff."

"In Leviticus 25, you told us to watch the moon and the days. You required from us a Sabbath day, a Sabbath week, a Sabbath month, and you even required from us a Sabbath year every seven years. Then you required from us a Sabbath year of years—every 50 years—called Jubilee. In Exodus 12, it was you, God, who gave us detailed instructions about how we were to celebrate Passover on the new moon, every year, regardless."

"So who asked for all this? You did. These are your rituals! And since Jesus has come, we also observe daily prayers, weekly worship on Sunday, and baptism. We want to be obedient, so we have a table set before us regularly with wine and bread. That's ritual stuff you told us to do. I guarantee you if we stopped doing this stuff, that would make you mad! But, I hear you, God. I hear you telling us in this text that it angers you when we just go through the motions as obligations that are not really an outpouring of love in our life. We treat them more as a duty week to week, day to day, year to year, rather than doing it out of relationship. You want this to come from the heart."

But if we aren't getting all "this" stuff right, why are you giving us more stuff to do? If we are not doing the rituals from the heart, then why do you think we are going to do more things from the heart? In verse 17, you give us more! You tell us to learn to do good, seek justice, rescue the oppressed, defend the orphans, and plead for the widow. It is more stuff to do. Look God, if you want me to do it, I'll do it. Just tell me exactly how much you expect so I can get it right. How many days do you want me to work with the oppressed, how much money do you expect me to give the children, and how many hours do you need me to spend advocating for or visiting widows? Just give me a checklist and let me get it done because it looks like I've got a lot to do. I do want to please you and I don't want anything to slip, so how much do I need to do to just get by?"

"Okay, now I really get it. That first part about all of the rituals and offerings and worship and festivals is about loving you, God, with our heart and our soul and our mind and our strength. That second part, about doing good by seeking justice, helping the oppressed and the orphans and the widows is all about loving our neighbor as our self, isn't it? These are your greatest commandments. To love the Lord your God with all your heart and your soul and your mind and strength and to love your neighbor as yourself. You don't want either one of these kept out of obligation. You want them kept from the heart. You want us to feel our love for you and feel our love for one another. You want love to be the motive. I kind of understand that the people of Sodom and Gomorrah operated out of greed and self-seeking desire and they really didn't love you and didn't love each other appropriately. Okay, I get it. So, God, give me the strength and desire to love and to serve you well this day and to love and serve the people who cross my path. Amen."

Step 11: Sought through prayer and meditation to improve our conscious contact with God, *as we understood Him*, praying only for knowledge of His will for us and the power to carry that out.

Usually when we think of prayer and meditation we think of sitting quietly by ourselves with a lit candle, or kneeling beside our bed, or striking some other familiar posture of prayer. But I want you to know that most of this chapter is an example of prayer and meditation—seeking conscious contact with God, wanting to know what His will is and asking for the power to carry that out. Prayers can take many other forms besides the more familiar spontaneous prayers from the pulpit, well-known written prayers, and the Lord's Prayer. Sometimes our prayers and meditations with God are going to be filled with tears and anger. Sometimes they are going to be filled with gratitude or anxiety. Sometimes our prayers are going to be a flat out argument! Prayer also happens when we read a text from God's Word and we begin to struggle, wrestle and argue with it. Prayer happens when we try our best to figure out what God's will is for our lives and ask God to give us the strength to carry it out. Prayer takes many forms.

A rector at St. Phillips Cathedral in Atlanta recently wrote about a series of conversations he had with one of his parishioners. He was approached by a new parishioner who was a rough, salty old fellow. The parishioner said, "Father, can you teach me to pray?" So the priest set up an appointment for him to come in and learn how to pray. At the appointment, he talked to him about Orthodox breath prayers, the Lord's Prayer, prayers of the hours, prayers of thanksgiving, and all the prayers he could think of. Finally, with an almost dumbfounded, confused, sad look on his face, the parishioner said, "Usually I just get up in the morning and say, 'Thank you,' and when I go to bed at night, I say, 'I'm sorry.' I must really be doing this wrong." The priest then realized and affirmed that he was actually doing quite well.

Step 11: Sought through prayer and meditation to improve our conscious contact with God, *as we understood Him*, praying only for knowledge of His will for us and the power to carry that out. Sometimes that means getting into an argument with God. Sometimes it's as simple as waking up in the morning and saying "thank you," and going to bed at night and saying, "I'm sorry." It really doesn't matter how we do it. It just matters that we do.

Songs in the Key of Life

Isaiah 5:1-7

STEP 12

Having had a spiritual awakening as the result of these Steps,
we tried to carry this message to others, and to practice these
principles in all our affairs.

*Let me sing for my beloved my love-song concerning his vineyard: My
beloved had a vineyard on a very fertile hill. He dug it and cleared it of
stones, and planted it with choice vines; he built a watch-tower in the
midst of it, and hewed out a wine vat in it; he expected it to yield grapes,
but it yielded wild grapes.*

*And now, inhabitants of Jerusalem and people of Judah, judge
between me and my vineyard. What more was there to do for my vineyard that I have not done in it? When I expected it to yield grapes, why
did it yield wild grapes? And now I will tell you what I will do to my vineyard. I will remove its hedge, and it shall be devoured; I will break down
its wall, and it shall be trampled down. I will make it a waste; it shall not
be pruned or hoed, and it shall be overgrown with briers and thorns; I
will also command the clouds that they rain no rain upon it.*

*For the vineyard of the Lord of hosts is the house of Israel, and
the people of Judah are his pleasant planting; he expected justice, but
saw bloodshed; righteousness, but heard a cry!*

Isaiah is one of those prophets who incorporated song into his sermons. He sings while he is preaching and while he is writing. Every

once in a while I will sing a line of a song or chorus during the course of one of my sermons. Inevitably, someone exits the sanctuary and says to me, "Hey, keep your day job!" I know I'm not much of a soloist, but like Isaiah, I've been fortunate to work with some friends in the past and compose a few songs along the way. Most of us have a song or two inside of us.

Several years ago, I participated in writing a nativity drama complete with music. Before that, I had written a couple of choral cantatas and youth cantatas. I like the songwriting process. I also like to be around people who compose music. I have a lot of respect for them, particularly if they do it well. Maybe that is why I'm intrigued by Isaiah 5. I think Isaiah gives us a glimpse of how this sacred moment works in the very personal art of songwriting. He begins by saying, "I'm going to sing to my beloved a song about my beloved and his vineyard." All good songs start with inspiration. For songwriters, inspiration is usually the result of observing, hearing or feeling something that moves them to song. So Isaiah says, "I'm about to sing a song to my beloved about my beloved and his vineyard." Isaiah had an insight into God's heart. He had observed God's work in the world, God's feeling, and God's struggle with the nation of Israel and Judah. So he decided to write a song about God's actions. Isaiah was inspired by what he saw, observed and felt.

My favorite songwriters are those who write out of their own experience. When you hear one of their songs you just know that it is personal. Whether you love Jimmy Buffet or not, when you hear one of his songs, you know he lives down in The Keys. Most of his music is from the heart. Many people love the song "Pirate Looks at Forty" which is one of those autobiographical tunes that emerged out of his own heart and life. It begins with the words: "Mother, mother, ocean; I have heard your call; wanted to sail upon your waters since I was three feet tall." That is Jimmy Buffet. This is his experience of life.

You can tell when a musician is inspired and has experienced the music, rather than just performing the music. I love Charlotte Church and I remember seeing her perform on television when she was about 15 years old. Her performance was flawless. She could sing a song without any catch in her voice, even though the words spoke of all the emotional pain in the world—it was a perfect performance. To me, she seemed too young to have experienced the depth of the words that she was singing.

But, Isaiah says, "Let me sing for my beloved a love song concerning his vineyard." When you hear Isaiah's song, you know he is inspired. He is in touch with God's heart and feelings. Isaiah gives attention to God's ways in the world. This song is inspired. And, this song is honest and real. Isaiah doesn't clean up what he sees in the fields. He doesn't put on rose-colored glasses and he doesn't try to write a gentle song or chorus to make the world feel better—the song is just honest. So when you listen to the words of the song in verses 1 through 3, God digs, clears, builds, plants, protects, expects and loves his vineyard. That is what Isaiah sees. In verses 4 through 7, God has to judge, devour, break, trample and withhold. Isaiah sees this also. Isaiah gives us both the wonderful words and the difficult words. His song is honest and real when he writes about God's work in the world.

The first a cappella song to reach number one on the pop billboard charts was Bobby McFerrin's 1988 hit, "Don't Worry Be Happy." I have never liked that song. It tries to lilt us away from the honest pains of life and it just doesn't feel like an honest song to me. I like Bobby McFerrin. I just don't like the song.

On the other side of that coin, there was the eleventh album of Marvin Gaye that he produced by himself. Do you know why? It was because Motown didn't want to produce the album. Part of the album expressed a protest of the Vietnam War. And when Motown executives heard it, they said, "People don't want to listen to message songs, they just want to feel good." The public proved the marketing executives wrong. They wanted to hear a message and not just feel good. They needed something honest and real.

Historically our hymn writers have tried to be honest and real when they observe God and God's work in the world. A person once commented to me about hymnals, saying "As long as it has 'The Old Rugged Cross' in there, I'm okay." That hymn is an honest one. It says, "On a hill far away, stood an old rugged cross, an emblem of suffering and shame." It is not cleaned up a bit. It is just honest.

We have all been drawn to the lyrics of Horatio Spafford, an American lawyer, who lost four of his daughters in a sinking ship cruising toward Europe. As a result of that tragedy, he penned a hymn that we want in all of our hymnals titled "It Is Well With My Soul." It is another real and honest hymn that people of faith have loved and shared for many years.

What makes Isaiah's song so important is that it is not just inspired and honest, but it is a song to be shared with others. In this holy text we are invited to read, sing, feel, and question it, and wonder how God is working in our world today. We are asked to join in this song.

Do you remember the old Coca-Cola commercial that featured the song, "I'd Like to Teach the World to Sing?" In the beginning of the commercial there is one person singing who holds hands with one other person. By the end of the sixty-second little commercial segment there is a line of people holding hands all around the globe singing, "I'd like to teach the world to sing in perfect harmony." As that song was shared, others naturally wanted to join in. Of course, that is not just true for commercial songs.

In the Broadway musical, "Rent," one of the lead characters is diagnosed with AIDS. He is sitting in a room, all alone in a little apartment, thinking over his fate in life. A friend encourages him to attend a support group for persons suffering from that same particular disease, but like most people, he is hesitant to go. So, in the play, he is sitting in a window all by himself while the support group is meeting elsewhere. Then one person in the support group stands up and starts to sing a song with just three lines, *"Will I lose my dignity, will someone care, will I wake tomorrow from this nightmare?"* He sings it over again and then another person in the group stands and sings with him and another and another and another until, finally, everyone in the group is standing and singing those three lines together. The lead character then steps out of the window in his apartment and walks over, joins the group and sings with them.

Step 12: "Having had a spiritual awakening as the result of these Steps, we tried to carry this message to alcoholics, and to practice these principles in all our affairs." AA groups and recovery groups don't just have Twelve Steps. They also have twelve traditions. The steps are about our personal recovery. The traditions are about how we function together as a group of people. Tradition 11 says that our public relation policy is based on attraction rather than promotion. People in recovery—AA, Al-Anon, NA, OA and other recovery groups— sing a song as best they can...one that is inspired by experience. It is a real and honest song even when it is difficult. People who find themselves in need, with the same kind of needs, are invited to join the song and sing freely. What a beautiful expression of the gospel.

In the gospel of Matthew we read what is commonly referred to as, "The Great Commission." I'm convinced that recovery groups have a lot to teach us about how to share gifts. Songwriters have a lot to teach us about sharing gifts as well. As Christians, we have observed God's work in our lives. At times it has felt joyful and other times it has been difficult. But when we share our experience honestly and openly, it is a story or a song that we invite other persons to become a part of. It is an experience of attraction rather than promotion.

I remember when Mark became a Christian. We grew up in the same church and were part of the same youth group. He was the roughest kid in our youth group. He got sent home from every youth camp we ever attended. He was expelled from school multiple times. At camp one summer, the preacher ended his sermon with a song that had these words in it:

> "I don't know what a sinner you are, but I know what a savior he is. I don't know where your feet have carried you, but I know his walked up Cavalry's Hill. I don't know what kind of words you've spoken, but I know his words were, 'Father, forgive.' I don't know what a sinner you are, but I know what a savior he is."

Mark made a profession of faith that night. On the last night of camp, as we all sat around the campfire crying and sharing our testimonies, Mark was in tears. Our youth minister asked, "Mark, what prompted you to make that decision?" and he just said over and over again, "It was the song; it was the song; it was the song." Inspired. Honest. Inviting.

Come join the song.

Andy Anderson
INSTITUTE

This publication was made possible in part by funding from the Andy Anderson Institute. Your tax-deductible donations to the Andy Anderson Institute allow us to:

1) Maintain a comprehensive database of local, state and national family care professionals and treatment centers.

2) Plan, implement, and sponsor conferences that train and encourage faith professionals, family care professionals, and the community at large.

3) Publish and distribute resources—like this one—for the strengthening of families and encouragement of family caregivers.

4) Explore and implement avenues of assistance for struggling, determined families.

You can learn more about the Andy Anderson Institute by calling Jim Dant at 478-737-7298. You may send your donations made payable to:

The Andy Anderson Institute
P. O. Box 250
Macon, GA 31202

CPSIA information can be obtained
at www.ICGtesting.com
Printed in the USA
BVHW092048080222
628188BV00008B/270